WHILE I BREATHE, I HOPE

A FAMILY'S BATTLE WITH COVID-19
THE STORIES OF THE MIRACLE THREE

KEVIN SHORES

authorHOUSE®

AuthorHouse™
1663 Liberty Drive
Bloomington, IN 47403
www.authorhouse.com
Phone: 833-262-8899

Published by AuthorHouse 02/03/2023

ISBN: 979-8-8230-0004-8 (sc)
ISBN: 979-8-8230-0003-1 (e)

Library of Congress Control Number: 2023901677

Print information available on the last page.

CONTENTS

DEDICATED TO

All the RN's, CNA's, Doctors, Occupational and Physical
Therapists, Case workers and ECMO Technicians from:
St. Mary's Hospital of Madison, Wisconsin
University of Wisconsin Madison TLC
Freeport Memorial Hospital
Monroe Hospital
Select Specialty Hospital (Madison)
Van Matre Encompass Health Rehabilitation Institute
Without you we simply wouldn't be here.
Thomas Alan Shores
(April 10, 1950-February 2, 2022)
Copyright 2022 by Kevin J. Shores
All rights reserved
For information about permission to reproduce
selections from this book, Write to:
Kevin J. Shores
1110 S. Adams Ave,
Freeport, IL 61032
Or e-mail to:
kevinshores61032@gmail.com

INTRODUCTION

Welcome to our little piece of family history. Multiple people have contributed to this compilation and thus different formats were used in the writing. As you go from person to person you will notice the style of each of them will be different. It gives each person the ability to tell their story in their own unique way.

There are family members and friend's names mentioned during the stories who don't have direct involvement but play parts that contributed to the stress levels and hectic lives some were under during our hospital stays.

The stories here have been compiled by researching all of the notes, texts, Doctors meetings and briefings, WebEx calls and in Kevin's case from his personal journal he started the day after he woke up. This is how he managed to capture the details so clearly. Erin's delusions stuck with her to the point she could recreate them on paper as well. While Kevin was at Select, he and Erin decided they would combine each of their stories together in written form should family or their caregivers be interested in knowing what went on in their heads. And if they didn't at least we would have a record of it and benefit from it therapeutically.

FAMILY INTRODUCTIONS

Kevin – Father of Erin, Haley and Ethan/ Husband of Dorene

Dorene – Mother of Erin, Haley and Ethan/Wife of Kevin

Erin – eldest child and daughter of Kevin and Dorene/ wife of Joshua (Josh)

Haley – second eldest child and daughter of Kevin and Dorene

Ethan - youngest child and son of Kevin and Dorene

Joshua (Josh) – Husband of Erin

Aurora – Fiancée of Ethan (now wife of Ethan)

Samantha (Sam) – "adopted" daughter of Kevin and Dorene/ "twin sister" to Haley, "sister" to Erin and Ethan

Bob – Brother to Kevin

Gary – Dorene's Father

Joanne – Dorene's Mother

Chad – Dorene's brother

Rusty – Joanne's cousin- (never married, no offspring)

ERIN

PREFACE

This is my story; the story of my battle with COVID-19. This is true, and the details provided are given to the best of my ability. These events have been pieced together for me by family, friends, chaplains, and medical professionals that took care of me when I was sick.

It documents my journey from diagnosis through therapy. I have been so incredibly blessed this last year. It has been the hardest thing I've ever had to physically endure and heal from, but I'm so grateful to have the opportunity to get well. So many did not have this opportunity. God honored the prayers of my family and friends and brought me through this virus whole.

Now the air seems lighter, the breeze smells sweeter, and love feels stronger. I've found a new joy in this second chance to live. I know there's a reason I'm still here; a reason God saved my life. I think a huge part of this reason is to show people that God is still the God of Miracles – my family and I are living proof of this! God is the Great Physician, and no matter what the doctors' reports may say, He has the final word! And thank goodness for that!

I hope you're able to see God's Glory in this story, and how He played such an intricate part of our survival and healing. He is the reason we are still here, and the reason we exceeded all expectations every step of the way. Thank you, God, for making a miracle of my life.

DIAGNOSIS

This whole story began on June 10, 2021. We got together for my brother and sister's birthdays (Their birthdays are June 9 and June 10). Little did we know at that time, something sinister was lurking among us.

Over the next two days, I felt congested and had a little harder time breathing. I thought it was allergies and maybe bronchitis, as I used to get bronchitis several times a year.

On June 12, we got together at my brother Ethan's house for a barbecue, as he was excited to show us his new house and grill out for us. This day, I received my first clue that something was wrong.

When Ethan brought in the hotdogs he'd grilled, I realized I couldn't smell them. Anyone who's ever eaten a hotdog knows that you can smell them cooking a mile away, so I knew that if I could not smell them right under my nose, there was a problem.

Still, I was not too concerned, until I started to feel feverish. I was suddenly freezing and clammy when the air conditioning kicked on, which is not something that is normal for me. I am the queen of air conditioning, as I am always warm.

By June 13, I was finding my chest felt constricted and I felt that I needed to be checked out. My husband Joshua took me to the ER (the doctors' office and Urgent Care were closed at this time) to get checked out, where the doctor on call diagnosed me with bacterial bronchitis. However, they did decide to do a COVID test, just to be sure. I was prescribed a Z-Pack and was sent home.

By the next morning (June 14), the results were in - I received an email via MyChart, stating that I was positive for SARS-COV-2. My first thought was "Well, crap." I immediately texted my job to let them know that I would not be in until I had healed from the virus and alerted my family members I'd been around to the situation.

By that evening, I had a fever over 102 that I was unable to get to go down, despite medications and cool compresses. Joshua took me back to the ER, after I called ahead. They brought me in and kept me, admitting me to the COVID wing of the hospital with low Blood Oxygen Saturation. The doctor must have noticed I was sicker than I realized, because he asked me if I had a POA or Living Will. This scared me.

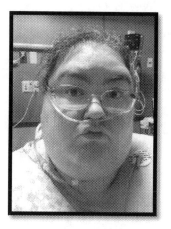

Me in the hospital before being transferred to the ICU.

I told him I had a POA but needed to have it updated so my husband was my primary Power of Attorney, and my Mother was my Secondary. I did this so that if something were to happen to me, the burden of my care would not be on one person's shoulders alone. This also gave my husband someone to lean on in case tough decisions needed to be made.

The doctor said I needed to have a meeting with my family to discuss my wishes as far as my healthcare and such. He brought in an iPad, and I vaguely remember talking with my family about what I wanted to do. I made it clear that I wanted to live, and that all measures to make this happen should be employed, if needed. This is the last thing I remember, and even that is foggy.

It wasn't long before I was in Hypoxic Respiratory Failure/ARDS. I was moved to the ICU on June 15th, where I continued to decline rapidly. My blood oxygen saturation was between 30% and 40% for several hours.

But here is where I encountered an amazing RN, named Sam. Sam took care of me while I was scared, and he prayed with me before I was placed into a coma and intubated. I know that must have brought me so much comfort at perhaps the scariest moment of my life to that point. I am so grateful to him for this.

Sam, Josh, and Erin
(pictured post COVID-19 hospitalization)

INTUBATION AND COMA

Most of what I know from this point on, until I woke up, I learned from medical records and medical professionals who cared for me while I was ill.

From what I was told, the process of my being intubated took two hours, and it went "horribly." Even after intubation, my oxygen saturation levels were not going up, despite the vent being at 100%. It was determined that I needed to be flown to another hospital that would be better able to help me, as they had done all they could for me.

There had been discussion about my being put on ECMO, but it was determined I was not a candidate because of my size. I was then flown to St. Mary's Hospital in Madison, Wisconsin, via medivac helicopter on June 16th. From what I've heard, it was pretty touch and go, and they were concerned that I may not make the 20-minute helicopter flight to Madison. Upon arrival, my blood oxygen saturation was still only around 50%.

My family was told not to plan for more than a day ahead at this point, as it was unlikely that I would survive; and, if I did manage to survive, I would likely have permanent brain damage due to my lack of oxygen for so long.

My Mom was somehow able to see me through the window in the door to my ICU room and was informed of how critically ill I was. They also called my husband. At some point, they had my mom and Sister Haley call me to say goodbye.

DREAMS AND DELUSIONS

During the time I was in a coma, I had several dreams and delusions. These dreams were SO real, that I thought some of them had really happened. This affected me more than I realized. I've been remembering them bit by bit.

Big Investment

I bought a hotel in Florida. It was a tall skyrise type building with a carport below. It was an unusual building. The bathrooms were at the side of the rooms, and the showers were behind the mirrors. The water would spray out from around the mirrors. There was no bathtub or real shower. Just a chair built into the wall and a single drain in the floor so the water could escape. I decided to live there, and soon realized there was an elderly couple also living there with their granddaughter. They must've been staying there when I bought the hotel from the previous owners.

Sun and Sand

I went to the beach on the coast and put my feet in the warm water. It was so comforting to feel the waves lapping around my ankles in a white foam as I stood looking out over the ocean. The breeze wrapped itself in a salty blanket around my skin, and the scent of the water filled my nose. The sun was warm on my face. I felt such peace there. I sat down on the tepid sand at the edge of the water, listening to the birds and the waves, and closed my eyes, allowing my senses to be open to the beauty I was surrounded by.

Cruisin'

I found myself downtown in a large city. I was driving a large, white convertible with a girlfriend (a person I've never met in real life, but a friend in the dream). It was a beautiful, sunny day. As we drove around, we came to a part of the city I didn't really recognize but had a bad feeling about. I looked to the sidewalk, and next to a chain-link fence stood three men. Two of the men (I couldn't see their faces or get a good look at them as we drove by) were speaking with another man. Suddenly, gunshots rang out, and I look over to see the single man grasping at his stomach. He collapses as the other two men run off.

We're Fancy

I was staying in a hotel, but I was sleeping by the kitchen/cafeteria area. I could smell the delicious coffee creamer. Looking back, I think I was smelling the breathing treatments they were giving me, as those had a sort of hazelnut smell to them. it wasn't half bad!

Upon waking at the hotel, I tried to stand up and ended up falling face first into a trashcan. I was too weak to get myself out of it, so I was calling out for help. Out of nowhere, my boss, Laurie, came to the rescue and pulled me up and out of the receptacle.

After that, we decided to go shopping. We were on the hunt for designer gold earrings and lapel pins. We were feeling fancy!

Big Purchase

I dreamt that I had sold the house we are currently living in and bought a new one. Apparently, I was Mrs. Money Bags in my dreams!

The Great Escape

I was in the hospital, and I was having a discussion with the doctor, telling him that I needed to go home, because my mother had called and told me she needed me at home. I emphatically and passionately professed to the doctor that I didn't care if I had to leave AMA (Against Medical Advice), because my Mom NEEDED me! Mom came to get me, and we were both telling the doctor that it was important for me to go home!

Telefono

I dreamt I had called and spoken with my Grandma Jo. We had a lovely conversation. When I told my Grandma this once I woke up from the coma, she was tickled pink that I'd thought of her while in a coma.

Day Pass

I was staying in a hotel with my mom and Sister Haley. We were having a girls' night, as I had been given a day pass from the hospital to spend time with them; however, I had to be back the next morning for my treatments and medications.

Glamorous

I was in a long, flowing gown that glittered gold. I was working in a high-end retail store. I donned golden heels as I flowed through the store, past windows looking out over palm trees and rays of sunlight.

Beautiful

I woke (in my dreams) as a beautiful African American woman. My short hair and curls framed my face, and my skin was clear and smooth. I felt more gorgeous than I ever had before.

Rehab

I was at Van Mater in Rockford, in a water-filled pool. I was in the water with three women who were helping me move my arms and legs and keeping my head above the water. They were asking me all sorts of questions about my home set up, and if I had all the things I would need while I healed and completed therapy. This one confused me greatly, because when I woke up from the coma, I thought for sure I was at Van Mater receiving therapy. I found out that was incorrect pretty quickly.

Oops

I was being moved to another area via conveyor belt. There was a chain around my waist to pull me upwards to change my position. Suddenly, I'm dropped on my left shoulder, and I hear a woman's voice giggle, then gasp, and say, "Oops!" This one is interesting, because I was unable to move my left shoulder for three months after I woke up.

Go For The Jugular

A female nurse was talking to me while she was holding my head back and to the side. She says to me, "Hold still. This can be a pain in the butt." I can feel her pressing something into the side of my head and down to my neck. There is a feeling like a pinch, and she places something in the skin on the top of my head. Looking back at this, I have a feeling this was my brain's solution to having an IJ Catheter (Internal Jugular Catheter) placed in my neck.

Immobile

I had several dreams where I was unable to move my arms and legs. I think my brain on some level knew my body was chemically paralyzed, and it came through into my dreams. In one of these, I was outside in the cold weather in a big coat. My sister was suddenly there and pushed me in a grocery cart into the building, as I was unable to move. We walk through a large hallway that looks like it belongs in a hospital and walk into an Italian Restaurant. There, we are approached by some staff members in scrubs, and I am informed that I was being transferred to their facility to be cared for.

Some Like It Hot

I was in an Italian Restaurant, and for whatever reason, I was laying in the back behind the wall, high up. It was so incredibly hot, it felt like I was inside the oven. I wonder if this was when I had a very high fever. I had this dream more than once.

Ice Cold

I dreamt that I had been cryogenically frozen while I was sick and in a coma. They had to "thaw me out" once I was brought back to consciousness. This was soon debunked.

WAKING UP

I want to start this section by saying THANK GOD for His Miracles, because I am one! He literally saved my life and kept me whole. There is no medical explanation for my miraculous recovery – God honored the prayers of my family and friends and brought me through. I've never felt more loved by God and my community, family, and friends.

I woke up on July 2, 2021. I don't really remember waking up, but just suddenly being aware that I was awake. The first thing I remember is a male ICU RN named Phil exclaiming, "Erin! I'm so happy to see you awake! You were one sick girl, and you had us scared!"

Next, a female nurse came in and began to ask me a lot of questions. I think she was trying to gauge my mental capacity, since I'd been without proper oxygen for several hours. However, it would be another week or two before I cleared what I called the "Coma Cobwebs." During this "clearing," I lost time frequently, and never really knew what time it was or even what day.

The conversation went something like this (keep in mind that due to the intubation, I had no voice, and everything I tried to say was barely a whisper):

Nurse: Can you tell me your full name?
Me: Erin.. (I couldn't remember my middle or last name.)

Nurse: Can you tell me your date of birth?
Me: April... ? (I couldn't remember the day or year.)

Nurse: Do you know where you are?

Me: The hospital? (I had no idea which one, because I was already in a coma when they air-lifted me out.)
Nurse: Yes, you're at St. Mary's in Madison. Do you know what day it is?
Me: *Shakes head no.*
Nurse: It's July 2nd.

This is where I get my first big shock, as last I'd known, it was June 15th. I had spent 16 days in a coma. My next shock was when I realized I could not move anything from my neck down except for wiggling a couple of toes and maybe twitch a couple of fingers. I had no idea that being in a paralytic coma for that amount of time would result in the atrophy of all of my muscles.

I spent several weeks in the ICU on quarantine until I was no longer feverish or testing positive for the virus. I watched the 4th of July fireworks from my room, overlooking Monona Bay. I cried as I watched the fireworks from bed.

At one point shortly after waking up, I looked down and noticed a dent in my left ring finger. "Where is my wedding ring?" I asked the nurse. She looked down and said, "You know, I'm not sure. It's probably with Security. I'll check." Later on, either that day or the next day, my wedding ring appeared on my tray in a specimen cup. I sent it home with my Mom once she was able to come see me, so that it didn't get lost.

Sometime around July 9, they finally transferred me to a regular room. This meant full-body PPE was no longer required, and that I could have one guest per day! Phil, my ICU RN, gleefully raced me in my hospital bed down the hall, to the elevator, up a couple floors, around the corner, and to my new room!

I believe it was around this time that I found out about Josh and my Dad being critically sick. Fortunately, Josh was home on oxygen by this time, and was well on his way to recovery after nearly a month in the Monroe Clinic ICU and Hospital. Daddy, however, had been placed on ECMO, and was not doing well. At this point, he had been on it nearly a month, and Mom had explained that he'd gone downhill very quickly, needing to be intubated. FHN had then air-lifted him to UW in Madison. I felt comfort knowing he was only 8 minutes away from me. I have never prayed for anything as hard as I did when I found out Josh and Dad were seriously ill.

Over the next couple of weeks, I worked very hard with Physical and Occupational Therapy. Squeezy sponges, Therapy Putty, and Resistance bands proved difficult for my arms and hands, but I was making progress. I really loved how OT and PT came at the same time and worked together to target the whole body.

My Mom, Sister, Brother, and Grandmother all took turns visiting me whenever they could make the 1 ½ - 2-hour drive. It really helped getting to see family members – it kept the anxiety and loneliness at bay. I had been struggling with anxiety being in a strange place, after a serious illness, far away from my family and friends. This was causing my blood pressure to be much higher than normal, which led to them putting me on a 10mg dose of Lisinopril.

At this point, they gave me my first swallow test. They determined I could start eating some solid foods and honey thick liquids. Thin liquids, such as water, were still a no-go, as there was a risk of aspiration. My throat was still recovering from where the vent was. Because I had been intubated for so long, the hyoid bone in my throat was not moving correctly to allow for proper swallowing of thin liquids. I had to do exercises like sticking out my tongue and swallowing to work on making it become unparalyzed and able to move properly. I was SO happy to finally be able to drink something, even if it didn't exactly quench my thirst. Anything was better than a couple mercy ice chips a couple times a day!

I worked on my muscle "re-growing" over the next couple weeks, and then had my second swallow test. It was determined that as long as I tucked my chin, I was okay to try drinking thin liquids. I still struggle sometimes with thin liquids, but I have faith that this will heal and go back to normal.

Therapy at St. Mary's

They also began Occupational and Physical Therapy around this time. It was time to start correcting the severe muscle degeneration. Most days I saw Jane and Jerry, but there were other days when I saw Ashley, Carmel, and another lady (I wish I could remember her name). They are all AMAZING. I cannot thank them enough for all their encouragement and hard work to help me regain my strength.

We started with sitting at the side of the bed to strengthen my core muscles. We also practiced some bed mobility so I could roll when needed. Once I was able to sit up on my own, we began to work on my hands, arms, and legs.

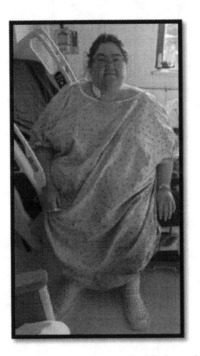

First time sitting up in bed by myself!

At this point, I still had in catheters and an NG Tube which fed me through my nose. I was also having to be hand-fed by CNAs, as I was unable to lift my arms. Once I was able to lift my right arm some, I could feed myself a little bit.

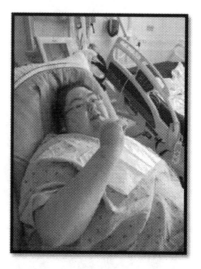

My first time feeding myself! It was really hard, and I could only lift my right arm a little bit at the elbow.

We worked first on my hands and arms. I had therapy putty to squeeze and pinch and was also given therapy sponges to squeeze. I was so weak I couldn't push the call button on my remote, so I was given an easy push that I only had to barely bump with my hand to send a signal to the nurses' station. I was able to regain some movement in my right arm and hand, and a small amount in my left hand.

Then, rehab began on my legs. They put me in a lift that reminded me of a Johnny Jump-Up that is used for babies and hangs in the doorway. They used it to help me relearn how to walk with a walker from the bed to the door, and then backwards, back to the bed. It allowed me to walk without having all my weight on my legs. It felt so good to stretch my legs and start to heal!

We also worked on ankle rotation and moving my lower legs out at the knees and control the movement both outward and when bringing it back.

Back to Monroe Clinic

On July 15th, we received word that Monroe Clinic Hospital had agreed to bring me back to complete my rehab. This was a relief, as my insurance would not cover a rehabilitation facility or even a nursing home for me to stay at while regaining my strength.

On July 16th, I was able to transfer from St. Mary's back to Monroe Clinic Hospital via ambulance. I was ecstatic to be able to finish my rehab so much closer to home. It was so much better for my mental health. Being able to see my loved ones on a more regular basis helped get me through, as I had been terribly homesick.

My wall of love!

The first time I saw Josh, it had been over a month since we'd seen each other, and I bawled. He had been discharged home on oxygen, Lovenox shots, and Warfarin (due to a couple PE's – Pulmonary Embolisms - they'd found after a CT scan with Contrast – we thank God for Kate Kinney, NP, who caught this!). He is now off the oxygen and his INRs are finally in a normal range. This has allowed him to discontinue the Lovenox shots! He would need to be on Warfarin for another two months to make sure the PEs were fully dissolved. An x-ray that was performed at the Pulmonologist's office revealed that his lungs were almost back to normal after that time period.

At this point in time, I was still unable to walk, and had limited mobility of only my right arm. Even feeding myself was a big challenge. I had to stick to just finger foods for quite a while.

To transfer me from the hospital bed to the chair (and vice versa), a lift was used. It was a sling that was wrapped around me, and then hooked to a machine on the ceiling. This machine then lifted me up in the sling towards the ceiling, and then the nurses could move me around the room via the tracks, and then slowly lower me where I needed to be placed.

Shortly after my arrival, they had me using the "EZ Stand" machine. This machine has belts that go around your back under your arms, and around the back of your knees. The belts hook to the machine, and you grab the handles on top. The nurses then use the controls to gently lift you. The machine helps lift you until your legs can take over to help you stand. Then, because the EZ-Stand is on wheels, I could be wheeled around to wherever I needed to go, like the bathroom, bed, etc. We used the EZ-Stand for quite a few weeks until I was able to stand and walk with a walker.

To work on standing, PT would put the gait belt around me, and have me practice sit to stands from the wheelchair to the walker. I needed a LOT of help at first. Both with standing *and* sitting back down. Ashley would help pull me up to stand after doing a 1, 2, 3 while rocking forward. Eventually, I was able to stand without assistance. This then led to my first steps with a walker, and Ashley holding onto the gait belt – Haley, my sister, got to witness my first whole 9 steps!

Eventually, I was able to go to the Inpatient Gym to start more rehabilitation exercises. I walked the length of the room and started using the arm bike to attempt to unlock my left shoulder. I really liked the arm bike! There were a lot of passive range of motion exercises, because whenever I tried to bring my left arm up straight, it would turn inwards toward my body instead of up toward the ceiling.

Eventually, with OT, I practiced standing at the counter and stacking cones with each arm/hand, while turning my upper body. I must admit this made me VERY dizzy, and I had to sit down until the room stopped spinning and the pressure in my head subsided. Then with PT, I would stand at the counter and work on leg lifts and side-steps.

I eventually graduated to the big Outpatient Gym in the main level of the hospital, so Ashley with PT would wheel me down, and I would typically start out on the Nu-Step machine. I LOVED this machine! It allowed me to move my legs like I was marching or using the stairs without putting all my weight on my legs. It was a great way to help build up my thigh muscles. After this, I would walk the length of the room with the walker, with Ashley following me with the wheelchair so I could sit once my legs couldn't go any further. Each day I tried to do more than I had the day before. If I'd done 5 minutes and 300 steps at level 5 resistance on the Nu-Step, the next day I would aim for 6 minutes and 400 steps at level 6 resistance. If I took 90 steps across the room, the next day I would aim for 110 steps.

I eventually started doing peg boards and weights in OT with Jackie. There was a small, foam board with holes in it. I would have to pinch the pegs that were in a plastic bin and lift them over the side of the bin without touching it (to work on lifting my arms up), and then would put the pegs in the holes on the foam mat. I did this with both arms/hands. These arm exercises were HARD! Especially for my left arm, which was not cooperating like the right one. That shoulder really did not unlock until closer to fall.

In OT, once I had done arm movements like curls, we added resistance bands and weights. My right arm was able to start out with 1 lb. for a few curls before my muscles gave out. The left could not – partly due to not having feeling in some of the fingers on my left hand. This caused me to be unable to close my fingers around the weight. We used resistance bands to build up strength until I was able to grip the weights.

With the weights, we not only did arm curls, but also wrist flexion exercises. Lifts, rotations, etc. Each week, my goal number of completed exercises would increase.

One thing I have noticed since waking up from the coma, is that I have new and increased neuropathy in the arch and first three toes on my right foot. It got REALLY bad in the hospital, but with my new medication regimen, it has improved. I also realized that I have no feeling in certain parts of my body:

- My right forearm
- My left lower back
- The tip and part of the right side of my tongue
- My middle and ring fingers and the thumb and part of the back of my left hand

- Parts of my feet
- Parts of my Abdomen

This could be because for 20 hours a day, I was in the same position on my stomach to help me breathe. They would then flip me to my back for the remaining 4 hours. I'm not sure if nerve damage can happen from that, or if COVID-19 can cause it. I asked my PCP, but he did not know. There just isn't enough known about it, yet.

In OT, we started doing cane exercises. I was able to assist my left shoulder in lifting the cane above my head. We also did what my husband called "gear shifting," where you would push the top of the cane forward and then pull it back. I am a firm believer that these cane exercises are a lot of the reason I can now lift my left arm above my head without wrenching my shoulder or having my arm turn in toward my body!

DISCHARGED HOME

I pushed myself hard so that I could be discharged as soon as possible. At this time, my Dad's health was not great, and my Mom was worried I wouldn't get the chance to see him in person. So, I spoke with my nursing team and therapists, and found out what I needed to achieve to be able to be released. I worked hard over the next week or two to accomplish those goals and was able to be discharged home on August 6, 2021. I had spent 53 days hospitalized.

My "I'm Finally Home!" Selfie!

My Mom and Sister came to pick me up, and little did I know the surprise that awaited me! As I was being wheeled out, the halls on the first floor and lobby were lined with doctors, nurses, clergy, volunteers, security, etc., who cheered and clapped for me as I left. I bawled; I was so touched!

VISITING DADDY

I was able to go up and see my Dad at UW's TLC Unit that following Wednesday, August 11th. But not before taking a tumble on my way out the door. I had not been used to walking with shoes on, and when I went to step through the door to the porch, my foot got caught on the door frame. My knee buckled, and down I went.

My Mother showed up shortly thereafter, and after a mild panic, she, my husband, brother, and sister attempted to get me up off the floor. I was still very weak and unable to get myself up, so I needed help. After a half hour of trying different methods to pull me up, my Mom ended up calling the fire department for a lift assist. They sent 5 big guys, and 3 smaller ones to help get me up off the floor. They used the gait belt and had me on my feet in .2 seconds. They put me in the wheelchair and got me to the car. Once I signed the paperwork, we were on our way! (Thanks, FFD!)

I had received special permission to be able to attend a meeting at UW with Daddy's current medical care team with my Mom, and then be able to see Dad in person for the first time in two months. He was awake when we got there, so I was able to talk to him.

The nurse asked him if he wanted to sit up to see me, and he shook his head yes. He kept saying in a whisper, "Help me. Out! Erin, help me. Out!" The nurse said he wanted to jump out of bed and leave – he'd been in escape mode all day. He was still so strong! He was lifting his arm and legs, despite being in a mostly sedated state for nearly two months!

I told Daddy I was going to anoint him and pray over him, and he let me. I anointed his forehead with anointing oil and held his hand while I called on the authority of Jesus Christ and declared and decreed accelerated healing over my Dad. I asked God to send angels to guard him, demanded the spirit of infirmity to be bound and cast back to hell where it belongs, and decreed new lungs and a new heart for Dad. He closed his eyes and held my hand until we finished praying. At one point he even took my hand and pulled it up onto his chest over his heart and held it there for a while. This did my heart so much good, as he then knew I was okay and could focus on his own healing.

After a while, the Dilaudid they gave him when he was uncomfortable and in pain began to kick in. He fell into a comfortable sleep, so I just sat with him and rubbed his arm as he slept. I was so thankful to be able to be with him in person, even if he was unable to communicate like he wanted to. I think it did both of us a lot of good. I continued to pray and believe in a miracle for Daddy.

RETURN TO MONROE CLINIC HOSPITAL

On August 14, 2021, I ended up back in the ER. I had been dealing with a sore under the skin in my right groin as a result of Hidradenitis Suppurativa and the inflammation from COVID. My body had been through a lot at this point and was having difficulty fighting off an infection. By the afternoon, the sore had gone from a small area to one the size of a baseball on the top of my thigh. I knew I needed to get to the hospital for IV antibiotics, as this was not my first rodeo.

I was immediately placed on Sepsis Protocol, as the residents on call that day were worried about either Necrotizing Fasciitis or Sepsis. This is because my blood work was showing high inflammatory markers.

They did a CT scan, which revealed a 4cm area with some air in it from the sinus tracts, due to HS. Dr. Huntsman, the general surgeon, believed this was a combination of HS and Cellulitis, and not something even more scary.

I was placed on IV antibiotics right away, and by the next day, the redness was starting to recede, and the pain was not as intense as it had been the day before. My white blood cell counts were also in a normal range, which meant the antibiotics were doing their job. Praise the Lord! This meant that we were on the right track, and that the diagnosis of cellulitis was correct.

The nurses saw me come back in and were like, "Erin! What are you doing back here again?" It had only been 8 glorious days since I'd been released to go home. It was definitely not how I'd planned to spend my weekend.

I woke up the morning of August 16th with a swollen face. It was very tight, so I was glad Dr. Patterson noticed it, too. It was determined that I had developed Cushing's Syndrome from the Dexamethasone steroids

I'd been placed on. My face was drawn so tight I could hardly open my eyes, and my molars were cutting into the inside of my cheek, resulting in a sore. A few days later I'd wake up to find bright purple stretch marks on my thighs and shoulders, too.

Cushing's Syndrome – Stretch Marks and Swollen Face.

I was so thankful for Josh, who came to visit me every day during this hospital stay. He kept me sane, as I was NOT happy about having to be in the hospital again. He brought me goldfish crackers for snacks, and we watched movies together. On Sunday, we watched Church together on my phone. He is such a blessing!

Eventually, the nurses were forced to stop giving me heparin shots, because every time they tried to give me shots, draw blood, or put in an IV, I'd bleed like a stuck pig. The admin, Angela, had to put in a new IV, and I literally had blood pour out of my arm and all over the tray.

So, after that, when I was laying down, I had to have my calves in these things that massage them to keep the blood flowing. It actually felt really nice; I just wished I could lay on my side with them on instead of my back. Sometimes laying on my back made it hard to breathe and hurt my tailbone (I've had three tailbone surgeries due to a recurrent pilonidal cyst).

I ended up staying in the hospital an additional 6 days, bringing my total to 59 days hospitalized. After that, I was sent home with oral antibiotics to finish getting rid of the infection.

DAD UPDATES

On August 15, my Mom called me to tell me that they had moved my Dad to another room (#5) in the UW TLC Unit. This room had a window. Mom and Haley drove up to UW so Haley was able to see Dad and sit with him. They wanted to give Dad more sunlight, since he'd been inside for so long.

They were also attempting to wean Dad down off ECMO again, but very slowly this time. This should hopefully give Dad's body and lungs the opportunity to adjust gradually instead of all at once.

As of the end of October 2021, Dad was released to come home! He had gone from UW's TLC unit to their COVID unit, to Select Specialty Hospital (which specializes in traches) which was also in Madison, and finally to Van Mater in Rockford, IL.

Visiting Dad at Select.

I'm so thankful for the medical personnel who took care of him and helped him to get prepared to be released to go home. He is truly a miracle!

KABOOM

Unfortunately, I fell a second time. I got up out of bed to get something from across the room, but the wheel on my walker caught the edge of my home hospital bed, and down I went. Knowing I was still not strong enough to get up off the floor myself, and Josh still recovering, too, he called for a Lift Assist.

The lady on the other end of the phone asked if I was hurt, to which he replied, "No, just her pride." Boy, was that true. I did NOT want to be lifted off the floor in my nightgown! Thank goodness the Lift Assist service is free, and the firemen were very nice about it! (Thanks AGAIN, FFD!)

OUTPATIENT THERAPY

By October 17, 2021, I was finally able to begin using 3 lb. weights in OT! I was also just starting to be able to take some steps without the assistance of the walker. My hips at that time were feeling pretty teetery. According to my OT therapist Chel, sometimes with extreme weight loss (I'd lost 53 lbs. by the time I was discharged from the hospital); the hips resettle in their sockets differently. This could explain why walking feels different to me now.

I was still getting pretty short of breath with activity. I was also still struggling with swallowing some liquids, especially thin ones like water and acidic ones like lemonades. They tend to irritate my throat. I have found though, that using a straw tends to help, as well as tucking my chin.

Once I'd been weaned from the Dexamethasone Steroids, I had a rebound reaction where all my joints began to be incredibly tender and painful. This has not ever stopped. It's worst in my hands, elbows, hips, and right ankle. It appears that my elbows, which have the worst pain, are suffering from Medial Epicondylitis.

When I started Outpatient PT with Joe, I found myself back on the Nu-Step machine. By October 18, I was able to do almost 1000 steps in 8 minutes at Level 4 Resistance. We then did marching steps and heel lifts while standing. Then, in a sitting position, I did exercises with the red resistance band to pull my legs against the bands, both from the front and the back.

Then, while lying on the table with my knees up and my feet flat, I did what are called "Bridges." Basically, you use your legs to push your butt up in the air off the table.

After this, it was side steps in the hallway at the railing. The best part was that I was able to do some of this unassisted, without a walker! While it felt amazing to be gaining more and more independence, I knew I needed to continue to be careful, and for longer distances, a wheelchair was still needed. Especially for middle of the night bathroom trips and the like. But every step was a little victory!

As time progressed, the exercises evolved and became more difficult. I could feel myself getting stronger with each passing week of therapy. By the end of November, in PT I was able to do over 1300 steps on the Nu-Step machine in 8 minutes at level 6 resistance. I did 5 sets of 4 stair steps, clam shells, bridges, heel raises, leg raises, and sit-to-stands (many of which doing two sets of ten each). I also started doing balance exercises like standing with my feet together on a foam mat, and then doing side steps across it. Once I'd done these a few times, I once again stood on the foam mat, and turned my head from side to side while still maintaining balance. I also graduated to the grey resistance band – the highest level!

In OT, I had worked my way up to a 5 lb. weight. I was also using green resistance bands and a weighted dowel rod as kind of like a dumbbell to lift both arms above my head, upward diagonally, and from side to side.

I also graduated from a walker to a cane for walking outside the house.

TELOGEN EFFLUVIUM

Around the middle/end of September, I started experiencing extreme hair loss. Within a couple weeks, I'd lost a LOT of hair. Every time I washed it or combed it; hair came out in clumps by the handful. I later learned that this distressing phenomenon was called "Telogen Effluvium." It is a somewhat common side-effect of having a severe case of COVID.

Because the hair loss was so noticeable, I cut my long hair into a shorter bob to prevent it from being pulled out. I invested in a hair care system called "Bio-Vita-Tin" that contained Biotin and Collagen to help prevent further drastic hair loss, and to promote healthy new hair growth. I bought hair, skin, and nails vitamins, as well as thick headbands, should I develop bald spots. I also got a super cute stocking hat, just in case.

October 18th's shower resulted in a "Chewbacca-Took-A-Shower" type hair loss situation. I knew it was just hair, but I couldn't help but cry as the hair just kept coming out. I felt physically sick to see it. I prayed for strength and for the hair loss to stop.

By the middle of November, the hair loss seemed to be slowing down some, which was a huge relief to me! Now I am just waiting for it to start growing back!

On a humorous note, I was talking to my Mom (Dorene) one day about Telogen Effluvium, and she gave me a confused look and asked, "What is that? A Christmas Carol?" I laughed and said, "Yes Mom, it's a Welsh Christmas Carol." Then I explained what it actually was.

CARDIAC TESTING

When I went in for the Cellulitis infection, my heart rate was VERY high, in the mid-to-upper-120's, creeping into the 130's. I'd been having heart palpitations and feeling flutters in my chest for weeks, along with dizziness and light-headedness. This, along with the new high blood pressure, caused some concern. Due to this, I went through some testing to see what was going on.

The first one was a Holter Monitor. It was a sticky pad that was affixed to my chest that could monitor my heart rate over the course of three days. It had detected some tachycardia and skipped beats, but it was determined that this was not something that was affecting my heart.

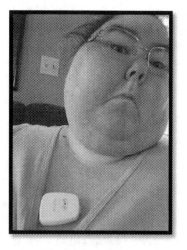

The Holter Monitor

I also had scans done to monitor blood flow, a Stress Test, and an Echocardiogram. After all was said and done, it was found that there was a bit of calcium on the outside of my left ventricle (this could not be corrected and was thought to be caused by COVID), and that there was a small amount of blood that was pumping upwards from my left ventricle in the wrong direction. However, the Cardiologist said that it was so minor it was less than miniscule. He said overall my heart was doing very well, and that I shouldn't have to see him again.

December 2021

I am ahead of schedule on my therapy, and I have completed my OT requirements. Chel told me at my last appointment on November 18, 2021, that I no longer needed to come in for outpatient Occupational Therapy. My last Physical Therapy with Joe and Julie was on November 16th, and he said it was my choice on whether I needed to add any on from there or not.

There are some other things that COVID has really messed with in my body, such as my menstrual cycle. The last cycle I had was in May 2021, and as of the end of November 2021, I had not had another.

My skin has been different, too. My skin literally started to peel off after I woke up from the coma. It took over a month before it stopped. There are also ridges in my nails from the time I was very ill.

Despite everything that has happened, I feel stronger every day, and I'm so thankful for all those who cared for me while I was unable to care for myself.

Every doctor, nurse, CNA, Respiratory Therapist, everyone who prepared and delivered meals to my room, my family and friends who are second to none – I don't have the words to express just how much their love and care has impacted my life. They went above and beyond to pray for us, love us, and provide for us in so many ways. From meal trains to gift cards and gas cards, to donations and funds, to fundraising, to visits, to greeting cards, video chats, texts and phone calls, I am beyond grateful for them all.

T-Shirt from T-Shirt Fundraiser

Even people who have never met us reached out to help us. Churches sent us generous and beautiful gifts along with many prayers for healing. Volunteers at St. Mary's made me a gorgeous quilt, and I was given flowers at Monroe upon my release. Clergy and nurses sat with me and prayed with me and comforted me when I was in tears. "Thank you" just doesn't seem big enough. And most of all, I thank God for bringing my family and I through this. God is SO good! And we are blessed by His mercy and grace.

June 10, 2022

It is now a calendar year nearly to the date when we were struck with COVID-19. We may never know what variant it was; we can only speculate - but one thing is for sure: Our lives are different now than they were before. But not for the worse.

I know for myself; I appreciate things so much more. I have a faith in God that is stronger now than before. A husband who has cared for me and has been there for me through my recovery and has fought the battle himself. We have rebounded physically and emotionally and spiritually and are thankful for each day we have. And thankful for the family we still have the chance to see and spend time with and love on.

Because we have a second chance to live our lives, we thought it would be good to pay it forward. We recently adopted a 9-year-old dog named Max from the local animal shelter, and he is amazing. He's the sweetest, funniest, smartest boy, and he brightens our days!

Josh returned to work last fall in late October, and I started back to work in late January once we had recovered enough to do so. I am thankful to be able to work from home, as I still have some lingering issues. But that won't stop me! I've learned that we are resilient, and with God's help, can recover and heal!

The Miracle Three!

God is the reason we are still here. He saved us, and I am so thankful. I pray that those of you who read this book can see His Works in our stories. I pray that you are healthy and safe. Thank you for reading our story, and God Bless You.

December 26, 2022

Today is the day after Christmas in 2022, the second Christmas since we were sick. This last year has been joyful, even in the trying times. I lost my 15-year-old dog, Brutus, in March of 2022. This was very difficult for me and my family.

But out of sorrow came joy. We adopted a 9 year old Shiba Inu/Rat Terrier mix from the local shelter. His name is Max, and he has brought us so much joy and love. He loves treat-treats, belly rubs, and snuggles in

Mommy's big comfy chair. He loves being around his family and getting to go for walks in the sun. He has truly helped heal our hearts.

My Mom and Dad recently celebrated their 40th Wedding Anniversary on November 20, 2022 – what a blessing it was to be able to celebrate them again this year! Each holiday and celebration has so much more significance and importance now, and we are so thankful for each day we get to spend together as a family.

That isn't to say there haven't been challenges. There are some lingering issues we deal with each day. For me, it's neuropathy in my arm, hands, and feet, as well as numbness in the right side and tip of my tongue, my left lower abdomen, and the left lower side of my back. Sometimes I still have issues swallowing thinner liquids like water, but it's nothing compared to where I was before. It still takes a bit more air than it used to for speech, but this is improving all the time. The brain fog and fatigue have slightly improved, which has been very nice since I've been back to work.

I feel like I don't take movement and speech for granted any more, either. Every day when I wake up and stretch my arms toward the ceiling or lift my leg to point my toe, I am thankful for the strength I have to be able to do so. Being able to speak to communicate what I need is such an underrated ability. Not being able to speak to tell someone what you need, and not being able to lift your arm to point at a word board makes it difficult to let someone know what's going on.

Some days PTSD takes hold and on those days I have to practice a little more self care, even if that means laying down in a quiet room or listening to some music that calms me down. I never realized before that PTSD could come from being so sick, but I have come to realize it was a trauma I experienced, not just with myself, but with my husband and father, too – not knowing what was going on with them and then finding out they'd also been very sick. This is something that I'm constantly working towards improving, and have made some great strides in recent months.

I am so thankful to still be here and am so grateful to God for bringing us through this. We are so incredibly blessed, and I am determined to live my life for God and to show others the love of Jesus Christ, as He has shown to me. Thank you for coming along on this journey with us. God bless you all.

KEVIN

(DAD)

"God saved you, it was not just medicine.
God has a purpose for you. You need to discover what that purpose is."

Dr. Zaher Qassem, MD

PREFACE

This is a true, real-life experience of the different stages of our journey through Covid-19. Delusions, confusion, and eventual clarity.

I was unable to find much that would represent humor during this journey. It will most likely be found as a bit dark and disturbing.

Having discussions with many medical professionals they showed a strong interest in reading my notes about my experiences while I was asleep, after I woke up and the road to recovery.

All I would say at the time was they were notes from what I experienced while asleep. I wasn't about to tell them that those experiences continued even after I had woken and didn't want them giving me any additional medications especially mind-altering ones. I wanted to clear my head on my own. This is a full account to the best of my recollection.

The medical professionals rarely and some never, get to hear or read about this type of medical phenomenon. Generally, these patients don't recover from the coma or the ECMO or as in my case survived them both. This interests them and I find they will probably be more interested in reading this before, let's say, family members. I have found lately my family found it too difficult to read or would just outright say they would rather not. I am hoping the medical profession can gain some insight on what these people like me are going through and if not, it was at least good therapy for me.

For me it was 92 days in ICU, 60 of which were spent in a drug induced coma. They said it was the record. 83 days on ECMO which I understand is another record. It is usually a one-to-two-week span with a low survival rate, so I have been told.

Covid-19 has destroyed families everywhere. I've been fortunate to have a family who refused to give up on me when the hospitals administration said they should.

How the family fought to give me a chance knowing that the remote possibility of survival also included not having any real quality of life. They thankfully were willing to take that chance; and did.

How many stricken with this terrible virus passed on because they didn't have the family and community support I have. That the families just took the advice of the hospital administrators. Thank God my family decided to fight for me.

I woke up 60 days after admission once Dorene convinced them to discontinue certain drugs I was allergic to and to end the hallucinogens. I still don't understand the need for the hallucinogens. They simply made my sleep become filled with scary thoughts and delusions. Once I woke up it would take another couple of weeks to get through the confusion of what I had just been through.

This short book is covering these dark days and my trek through various therapy hospitals and eventually adjusting to being home.

Everything here is a true account of these days to the best of my recollection. That's the scary part.

There are characters in this book from my delusions that still give me a chill. Some I can't revisit, and I have had others type from my original notes, so I didn't have to. For some time, I had to ask Dorene "Did this really happen?".

Dorene helped bring me back to reality. She was the only one I trusted knowing what my mental state was. Who knows what they would think if they heard these stories? I wasn't going to risk getting put on any additional drugs.

Dorene is my everything.

FREEPORT MEMORIAL HOSPITAL UNIVERSITY OF WISCONSIN AT MADISON-TLC

THE KILLING NURSE

June 19, 2021

At home I had been dealing with a persistent cough. This cough would be persistent throughout my hospital stay through to weeks after I would get home. I have had pneumonia in the past and even though I had a pneumonia shot I thought it was what I had. I never thought it could be Covid 19 since Dorene and I had been vaccinated May 15th and had practiced social distancing.

Dorene took me to FHN emergency where initial diagnosis was double pneumonia, so I'm told. My memory from here on is lost. In fact, much of my memory for the previous year had been lost.

I was surprised at how fast I spiraled down.

I'm not sure if I was given drugs right off the bat but this is when my delusions began.

My understanding is I spent 3 days in ICU at FHN. Unconscious, I was kept in the same prone position for all 3 days until I was flown to Madison.

My first experience with the Killing Nurse was when I was being wheeled through FHN hospital. This is what I believe anyway. It wasn't conscious thought.

I constantly saw her out of the corner of my eye as I was wheeled on a gurney from one place to another. This angry looking, middle aged nurse with shoulder length gray wavey hair and dark evil eyes that were fixed on me like she hated the fact that I was still alive and wanted to make sure I made it to the cold box. Dressed in a white and blue nurses uniform I would later date her uniform to back in the mid-1800s.

Though not exactly like this picture I'm sure there were many different variations on this version. This is relatively close.

Two men wheeled me towards a large vault like door. They opened the door to a dark room. I could feel a blast of cold air rush over me as it opened.

THE COLD BOX

As they rolled me into the cold box, I could see the Killing Nurse giving me the slightest of smiles as I was being passed off to the people in the box. She knew why I was being put there and what purpose it served.

When entering through the door I made a point of looking at my wedding band figuring if they were going to kill me, I wanted to be wearing it when I was buried. I looked down and all I saw was the impression where the ring had been. At first, I was very angry which then turned to profound sadness. This had me on the brink of giving up. This band represents everything my life has been based on.

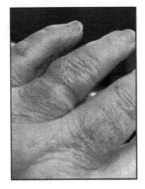

I was shoved along the wall just inside the door and strapped to it. The door slowly closed behind me as if it was goodbye. I knew my life was at stake but didn't know why.

The cold box had 3 people that operated it. Two up front, a man, and a woman and 1 man in back with me. It had the feeling of a shipping container and was painted black.

While in the cold box and looking out the other end of the box I was watching a woman tear a Johnny Knox Bears jersey down the back. My assumption was they were preparing clothing to bury me in. I thought to myself, I always wondered how they put clothing on a corpse. They must tear it down the back and lift the body up and wrap the clothing around them instead of struggling trying to pull things over their head and such. I can say I really don't know nor care to know how it's actually done.

Looking past the woman and the man there was a doorway out to a green lawn with a large hole dug. Sitting next to the hole was a cheap plywood casket on top of the pile of the freshly dug dirt. I said to myself "this is not how it ends."

I was upset first that they destroyed my jersey, but even worse, I wasn't going to be buried in a #13 Johnny Knox jersey. It was going to be a Walter Payton jersey or none at all.

Once shoved into the cold box I deduced this was how they were to put me to sleep. Patients that are likely not to survive are sent here to humanely put them to sleep though I didn't find it humane at all. My goal was to outlast their time limit. If I did that then they would have to pull me back out. For some reason I believed that time limit was 52 minutes. I shivered to the cold and watched the big clock on the wall count down. The face of the clock only had the number 12 on it and a minute hand that counted down. When the hand hit the 12 it was 52 minutes.

I don't know how or why but I survived it and the door opened, they then pulled me out into the warmth. I heard the man say to the two people he was handing me over to, "he made it".

I did it! I beat their first attempt at killing me. I made the decision at that point I wouldn't let whatever was going on with everything kill me.

Delusions

University of Wisconsin Hospital at Madison Trauma Life Center

THE JUDGE

I was pulled from the cold box, and it was a different place. Confused I started looking around and there she was, The Killing Nurse. Somehow, she managed to follow me. I began flailing. (I was told I had given the staff a lot of problems kicking my legs, lifting and pounding them to the bed. So much so they restrained them) Trying to convince the people moving me that she was looking for an opportunity to kill me, but I was unable to talk as I had been intubated and then vented. I wouldn't realize this until I woke up.

The cold box was what I believe to be my Med Flight from FHN to UW Madison. The 2 people in front were pilot and co-pilot. And the 3rd who was back with me was to make sure I stayed put during the flight. I was disappointed after I woke up that I didn't get to experience the flight.

I was taken to a room that looked to me as a judge's chamber. The judge figure ordered me to lay my penis on his table. I naturally resisted but his bailiffs held me in position. Looking at the table I see slivers of skin striking fear in me.

The judge then pulls out a cleaver and with 2 quick chops he shaves off any excess skin on each side. It happened so fast, and he was so accurate that there was no blood and the skin just fused back together. Looking back, I believe it was probably a nurse inserting my catheters.

I was then strapped down again on a gurney and sent on my way. Wheeling through low lit hallways I was eventually pushed into a room that appeared depressing and for some reason a little scary. I was then turned over to the doctor on call and another nurse. I didn't know nor have ever heard what the doctors name was.

At this point I apparently was having heart issues. Someone, I believe the doctor, hit me with defibrillator paddles to shock my heart into rhythm. This was incredibly painful. I was able to get the words out "don't ever do that again". Dorene says I had my heart shocked on several occasions and that a nurse named Peter was likely involved in at least some of them.

The pain of the shock was bad enough that it pierced through the sedatives and woke me up enough to respond to Peter. I don't know if this is reality or delusion. All I do know is I was shocked, and I am confident the pain I felt was real. I am not positive I was able to respond to Peter with my threat not being able to speak, though the event seemed very real.

Apparently in my flailing I managed to catch Peter with a solid punch to the chin that may have knocked him down. He was on my left side, so I imagine I caught him with my left hand. Fortunately, it wasn't my right hand because it would have resulted in much more significant damage. I was still at full strength at this point. Very muscular and 276 pounds. I don't remember doing this and this event has been described as a glancing blow to knocking him to the floor. Only Peter probably knows for sure. It may have never happened at all, and I was restrained simply because I was agitated. I would be interested to know for sure. I hope someday I get the opportunity to talk to him.

Word spread fast because many would bring it up after I woke up. I still have my doubts. I fought everywhere I went. I just couldn't make them understand the Killing Nurse was trying to kill me.

From this time on I found myself strapped down arms and legs.

LIAM

I was now in the ICU at UW Madison TLC. The Killing Nurse makes several appearances here. I fought to exhaustion. Unable to fight anymore I had to rest and accept the results should she get her chance. As the Killing Nurse was staring at me with those cold eyes from across the room a male nurse named Liam popped his face up right in front of mine. Liam would be in several of my delusions and with me when I woke up. He would ultimately become my first ICU Angel. I have no recollection of ever meeting or being introduced to Liam. I have no idea how I learned his name. But it seems I've known him all along.

He was wearing a protective hood like something out of a space movie, but I could see his face clearly. He had a weird smile on his face that was making me uncomfortable. The look on his face gave me the sense that he may be working with the Killing Nurse. I looked him right in the eyes and said, "I'll bet you are enjoying this, aren't you?". He just kept staring at me. Tired from fighting I just closed my eyes to rest. When I opened them a little later, they were gone. I would later realize it was all a combination of reality and delusion. The shocks to the heart were a reality. Seeing the Killing Nurse behind him was obviously a delusion, and striking Peter is still in debate. I later saw the same look on Liam's face when he was trying to make out what I was trying to say. He proved to me his ability to read lips was terrible and that look on his face came from his confusion trying to read my lips. I was unable to speak at the time of the encounter. It would be much later before I saw The Killing Nurse again.

Liam ended up caring for me while I was comatose along with many others. I remember hearing his voice occasionally comforting me and telling me everything would be ok, and that "he got me." I think the early times they took care of me set me up for a better recovery. I don't know what it was they did, but I would meet so many who would say they had cared for me during certain periods of time. I have heard that it's beneficial to speak to comatose patients. I personally found this to be true and comforting. I don't remember any actual conversations but believe they played a part in at least some of my dreams.

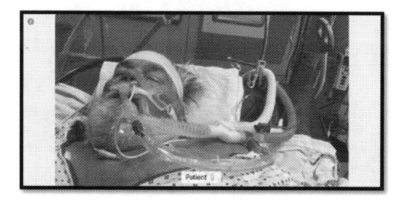

It was like a small army of nurses and CNA's. I can't say enough about the quality of people that UW Madison TLC ICU had. I wish I knew everyone's name. Many introduced themselves shortly after I woke up which was a problem. I was still trying to shake off the cobwebs from the sedatives and reality blended with delusion for at least a week and a half.

Delusions

June 21, 2021- August 31, 2021

THE THIEF

Delusion

The Thief is a relatively short woman, in her early 30s maybe. Very thin with a long bob hairstyle that was stark violet in color. She also struck me as a mean, vindictive person that lacked feelings, empathy, and class. A psychopath is another way to put it, I suppose. I can't stress enough just how disturbing this person is.

The Thief took everything from me. She manipulated Dorene out of basically everything we owned. I'm not sure how this happened since Dorene is the smartest person I know, but she did none the less. From our house to my car, she took it all.

She was allowing Dorene and Haley to occupy the downstairs in our home. It must have been part of the deal while she occupied the upstairs. With all her money, owning the building the TLC unit worked out of along with a bunch of other real estate in the area, I couldn't understand her living like this unless she had bigger plans. This was all very disappointing and disturbing.

I had several conversations with Dorene and Haley over WebEx or FaceTime or something similar where I asked them about the Thief and how the situation was playing out. They assured me they had everything under control and the Thief wasn't a problem. I still had a feeling I wasn't being told everything and they were trying to save me from the stress of the situation. I could see from the view the camera had that Haley had a mattress laid out on the floor in the living room. This confirming in my head that The Thief had in fact taken up residence in the upstairs. This was true and real that Haley's bed was on the living room floor but for other reasons. Mainly to be close to Dorene for comfort for the both of them and it remained there while she was sick later on in my hospital stay. I had seen this regularly they tell me over Webex calls, Haley's bed being on the living room floor, but I was unable to speak at this time so the conversations I thought I had must have been delusional.

Dorene and Haley said there were conversations over WebEx mainly because in the beginning I wasn't allowed visitors. They tell me they didn't understand much of what I was trying to tell them because of my inability to speak. They knew I was very agitated. They will explain this timeframe in their section of this book and hopefully detail it much better than I can. I don't remember much more than what I stated here.

Delusion

Freeport IL Home

At one point I was able to get a day pass out of the hospital to go by and check up on the house. As I drove up to the house and saw that the Thief had a large excavator tearing the house down. Erin was a half block behind me yelling "what are they doing to the house?". My response was "I don't know, where's mom?". I ran around the house to the garage area looking for Dorene. I came across 6 large radio flyer wagons each tied in tandem, one behind the other. In these wagons were 6 large orange balloons. I thought this was strange. As I got closer, I saw that there were faces and hands pressing from the inside of the balloons. There were children in the balloons. The Killing Nurse was at the lead end of the wagons with the Thief finishing up tying the last cart.

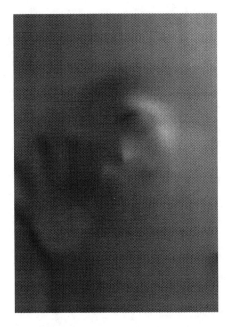

I yelled to them "what the hell are you doing?" The Killing Nurse yelled back in an old hag's voice, "we're taking them to market. You want to join them?" She then put the wagon handle down and began walking in my direction. I ran. I don't run from anything, but the Killing Nurse knew she had a definite advantage. I was afraid of her. I knew she had the ability to kill me.

I ran back around the house looking for a police officer or even just help. There wasn't a soul to be found. There wasn't a single car on the street. I looked and looked, and there was nobody around to help. I knew at this point I was too late. The children were lost. I didn't see the Killing Nurse after that until I saw her behind Liam in my room. Where she had made her last appearance. This also helped in my recovery not seeing her practically everywhere I looked. I could relax a little bit and focus much better.

I would later have a conversation with my daughter Erin about the Killing Nurse after I had gotten home. She gave me a whole new take on the Killing Nurse delusion.

After reading my notes she felt the need to explain to me what she thought.

She told me that she and Apostille Mike from her Church thought the Killing Nurse was a demon trying to take my soul and all the prayers over me and for me were so strong it kept her at bay. There were many who came in to pray over me.

The Killing Nurse scared me to the point of panic. It wasn't until she stopped appearing and I decided to rest, did she leave for good. A sense of calm came over me that allowed me to sleep in my delusion.

The next day I explained to Dorene the conversation Erin and I had. She remembered it well. Dorene had Erin work hard to be able to be released early from SSM Health Monroe, so she could see me a last time should I not survive. She told me how Erin had discussed my anxiety. How the nurses said I was unable to sleep but in short increments even though I was heavily sedated. The family explained this was normal for me not to sleep very much and sedatives rarely had any effect on me, but the anxiety was nothing they had seen before. Something was going on in my head. They knew some of the drugs were causing me problems, but Erin had a plan.

She came to visit me with prayer - a special prayer that Apostille Mike armed her with especially for casting demons out.

Erin asked me if she could pray with me, and I said yes. I don't recall any of this, but Dorene and Erin remembered it clearly.

Erin took my hand and began to pray with me. She finished her prayer and began Apostille Mike's prayer still holding my hand. Haley told me later that I stared at Erin with an angered look on my face throughout the prayer. Once she finished her prayers, I apparently slowly withdrew my hand and closed my eyes, falling straight into a calm sleep.

Was this God casting the demons out after Erin's prayers or was it the discontinuation of the drugs The Family was trying to get them to stop giving me? Was the angered look on my face the demon trying to scare Erin away and not complete the prayer? I consciously wouldn't stare at her like that. Then once the prayer was complete slowly and calmly drift off to sleep. Something to that point I hadn't done.

I have tried to piece together a timeline for this and according to Dorene, Erin came 2 weeks before they discontinued the bad drugs. There was a 3-day period in early to mid-August where they stopped the drugs to try to assess my condition then put me back on them.

My conclusion is Erin's prayer superseded the stoppage of drugs and therefore God had to be what cast the demons out. I began improving immediately and the Hospital took notice and began listening to Dorene and the Family. No more Killing Nurse pacing back and forth outside my room looking in or having The Thief scheming her next move to take even more from me. It also seemed as if all the struggles Dorene, and The Family had with doctors and administrators ended. There was harmony. So many roadblocks that they were continuously running into were disappearing. Dorene will expand on these in her section of the book.

So, when I had seen the Killing Nurse through the glass in my room and decided I was so tired I would sleep and accept what waited for me, it was God telling me it was ok, and He would cast the demons out of my body. I don't remember any of Erin's visit but don't think I really need to. I felt a calmness come over me and finally got some peaceful rest. It was like my mind was no longer obsessed with the thought of anything trying to harm me. I was finally at peace.

I would also later come to realize the orange bubbles the children were in were eerily similar to a daily chart that was posted on my glass wall and the curtains in my room carried the same pattern.

I remember opening my eyes and seeing Dorene. She was sitting beside my bed with 2 others standing behind her who appeared to be monitoring me. It was nice to see her as my eyes opened. This was my first recollection of waking up and actual clearish thought. Dorene asked me if I had an idea of the date. I responded no. Dorene tells me this had been done on several occasions previously, but this was the first I actually remember. She told me it was late August and waited for my response. I remember thinking to myself "ok, it's Summertime". I didn't realize all the time that had passed and really wasn't fully understanding where I was. She explained I was very sick and were now in the hospital in Madison. My thought was, ok, I'm not dead, so that's good. I was in a comfortable bed and many machines around me. I was confused by all of this, but Dorene was there, so I figured I was in good hands. It was weird that I knew I couldn't speak. But at the time it wasn't a concern. They were pretty much all yes or no questions. I must have given everyone what they wanted because they chatted as they were leaving, and I dozed off.

From that day forward I had an idea of what questions I would be asked each day so made a point of trying to find ways that would aid me in keeping track of the answers. I would get caught now and then with a new question but thankfully they were generic questions like a pet's name that were easy to answer.

I kept track of the day, year, and month by always watching for the shift change. Each time the incoming nurse would put her name on the board with the date. I watched that carefully because it was something I was having trouble with, and I needed to know if the nurse changed it or not so I could answer the question correctly. It was challenging at times making sure I was awake to make sure the date was in fact changed.

Once I gained the ability to speak by way of a speaker valve in my trach, and my mind began to clear. I began asking the questions. I asked Dorene about the Thief and her relationship. Dorene assured me that she had taken care of her, and all was good. I guess she was going along with the delusion to comfort me. She would be able to clear it all up properly once my mind wasn't so cluttered. She made me feel good again about everything. She would later prove to me that none of it was real. She chose to spare me from the confusion that it wasn't real. She just seems to know what to say and when to say it. Just one more reason why I love her so much. I'm a lucky man.

Delusions lingering into my waking up/ Confusion State:

My delusions continued during the time I was waking up and clearing my mind. It wasn't like waking up in the morning from a dream. It was more like falling in and out of dreams. Dreams so real you still questioned what really was real. Afraid to say anything I tried to keep conversations simple until I could tell Dorene about my problems and sort it out. I didn't want to give anyone a reason to keep me any longer than absolutely necessary. Dorene would ultimately get me through it. I did slip up a time or two but managed to cover my tracks. I remember telling my nurse Megan I had been a cop for a very short period of time, but it didn't work out. I would later come to realize that was a delusion. Luckily the topic never came up again, so I felt I dodged a bullet.

Delusion- Cats

At night I see cats. They are let loose to control the mice population. I can see them through my glass window out on the ICU floor coming out from behind equipment and through doorways once the lights were dimmed. It's like they have been trained to do this.

My rooms cat was white with a black masked face, black tail, and a large black spot on its back. It would come down the steps behind the machines. Slowly rounding the bottom of the steps. It never comes close to me. It always stays behind machines and in the shadows.

It promptly returns up the stairs once the lights on the floor get turned back up. They won't be seen now until tonight. This delusion was cleared up for me later but don't remember who cleared it up for me.

This person assured me there wasn't a cat in the entire building and, there wasn't any stairs behind the machines for the cat to come down.

This most likely was my nurse, Megan. I don't think Dorene ever brought it up so Megan would probably be the only one I would talk to about it.

This was going on at about the same time as another delusion around the 16th of September 2021.

I had asked Dorene to find the letter in a manilla envelope from the police department to see if it had any information on my compensation since I had been on administrative leave all this time.

Approximately a year prior to me getting sick I had joined the Police Dept. I thought it was Peoria but may have been Sterling. The delusion wasn't clear on this.

The third night being on patrol would be my final night.

Approaching morning just as the sun was coming up. I received a call from dispatch on a possible sniper situation downtown.

I sped to the address and discovered a man lying on the ground between two buildings with two fully automatic rifles on sniper stands. The ground sloped upward to where he was. He was lying behind one of them aiming at the street below.

I realized it was three minutes before 6 am when the night shift workers from that building would be pouring out into the street at shifts end and be sitting ducks.

I laid on the sidewalk with my elbows in the gutter for support as I aimed my weapon at the shooter.

I yelled for him to let go of the weapon and move away from it. He didn't acknowledge me and continued to take aim. I repeated the command two more times with no response.

The last command I gave him I told him I would shoot if he didn't comply. He ignored me.

I took aim at his right butt cheek. I knew I was out of time and people would be coming out of the door at any second. I fired one round and saw his hands drop from the gun. No other movement was detected. I stood up and started to cautiously approach the suspect when other cops began showing up. One was a supervisor, and one was a cop like me, named Mike. Mike was a tall black man in very good shape. Since I had only been on the force for three days, Mike was the only cop I really knew. Mike was impressed that I had hit the suspect shooting only one round and from such a long distance. In the real world I have had a lot of experience with long range target shooting with a pistol.

Mike told me to stay where I was as he cautiously walked up to the shooter. He checked for a pulse and pronounced him dead. This shocked me because I tried to shoot him in the butt cheek to keep from killing him. I asked myself what went wrong.

Apparently, my shot veered a few inches left and went between the cheeks straight up through to vital organs. The supervisor said I needed to surrender my weapon and head to the precinct to fill out a statement.

I went to the precinct, filled out the statement and was told I was on administrative leave and to turn in my badge. I gave him my badge and left his office. On my way out all the cops applauded me as if to say good job- that I had saved many people. I then drove home. I entered the house with Dorene sitting in her chair. She knew immediately something was wrong. She said, "You're home early". I said, "Yes, there was an incident". I explained what happened. We hugged and she assured me everything would be okay. I wasn't so sure.

It wasn't discussed again until the letter showed up.

Fast forward a year and a day or so before I am taken to the ER for COVID, a manilla envelope is delivered to the house from the police department I had worked for. I was still on administrative leave, so I was excited to see what was in the envelope. Having no intention of returning to the job, I was hoping it was all settled in my favor. Dorene opened it and pulled it about a third of the way out and read the first paragraph.

We are pleased to inform you that the matter of the discharging of your weapon resulting in the death of a suspect has been resolved and your actions have been deemed justified. This case is now closed.

Dorene then slid the paper back in the envelope and said that's all we need to hear right now.

Fast forward to September 16, 2021, believing I am thinking clearly, I tell Dorene to find that manilla envelope and see if I am getting compensated for my administrative leave since it ruled in my favor. She said she didn't remember any envelope. I told her from when I was a cop. I explained how we had read it when standing at the front door and to just look for it. She said okay and left for home. I would later say to her, "That wasn't real was it"? She said, "No, Honey. It wasn't".

I also learned later that these conversations were actually text messages, even though I thought they were in person. This was over three weeks after I woke up that I was still fading in and out of reality.

Delusions Polo, Forreston IL

Dorene had heard on the news that an entire block in Polo, Illinois had burned to the ground. This was a lingering delusion while trying to wake up. We both go to Polo regularly and enjoy everything from the restaurant to the grocery store to the chiropractor. So, we needed to see what block had been lost.

Earning a day pass from the hospital we arrived in Polo, we saw that it was in fact the block with the restaurant and other businesses, and they were reduced to rubble.

We began inspecting the rubble as we walked along the sidewalk from across the street. When we got about two thirds of the way down the block, I noticed something peculiar. The back end of a car was sticking out from the still smoldering rubble of the last building on the block. I walked closer and realized that it was my car that the Thief had stolen. All that was left was the back third of the car, the rest was just burned away. I knew it was Envy.

I remember the Thief remarking from her desk at the hospital that Envy had been stolen and she couldn't find another one like it. She was hoping insurance would give her enough money for a better car.

What's running around in my head is did she deliberately hide the car there then try to burn the building down? In trying to do so she accidently burned down the entire block.

When I saw Envy was a total loss, I became very upset. It was like losing an old friend. I always carried the title with me with the idea if I ever ran across her I had the proof she belonged to me.

I posted online that whoever had possession of Envy was welcome to the title and that I would be sitting on the bench across from the burned-out buildings with the signed title in my hand and wouldn't press any charges.

I pulled the title from my pocket and folded it over enough times that I could slip it between my ring finger and middle finger on my right hand.

As I was walking towards the bench, I began feeling very ill. I struggled to get to the bench. I put the title between my fingers and collapsed onto the bench. I hadn't eaten at all that day which was bad for my blood sugar.

While I was passed out on the bench, I heard the voice of my male nurse Liam say to me "Don't worry Kevin, I got you". I had no idea why Liam was there with us, I assumed he was traveling with us while I had a day away from the hospital. Soon after he said that I began feeling better. I thought he must have given me an insulin shot.

As soon as I woke up on the bench, I checked my hand for the car title, and it was gone. I popped up and began searching all around me, but the car title was gone. I asked Dorene, Liam, and passersby if they had seen anyone pass by and go near me, but nobody saw anyone.

I then sat back on the bench because I found myself unable to stand or walk. Dorene and Liam were sitting at a round table about 30 feet from me. I yelled to them I needed an ambulance to get me back to the hospital. They acknowledged me with a nod and continued their conversation.

It's now beginning to get dark and no ambulance. I yelled over to Dorene, "did you call for an ambulance?". Her reply was "No, you don't need one". That's because at some point, I must have blacked out and had been shipped back to the hospital while I was unconscious. I was looking around from my hospital bed at my room. They were preparing me for something. I was leaving and heading towards a new room. Upon arriving to my new room, I wondered why I was moved when the rooms were identical. I hated the design because I knew the Thief had designed the rooms. After all she owned the building.

I was surrounded by people wearing protective gowns, masks, and face shields. I believe this to be my first experience from the hallucinogens. I didn't like it. Reaching for a brown metal box sitting on a steel cart. My hand just melted through the box and the cart as if nothing was there. I closed my eyes hoping it would all stop.

Dorene and my family battled with the doctors on several occasions about the narcotics I was being given. One of which was known and in my file that I was allergic to. She will explain in her section of this book on just how heated and long these battles were that took place.

Eventually my family must have worn them down because the medical staff discontinued them. I woke up shortly after this and thus began the confusion stage. Erin would have another take on this later on.

I would continue fading in and out of my delusional state with consciousness for weeks. This must have been very difficult on my family and the staff. I'm not sure of all the problems it might have caused but like with the Military Man, I am sure this period had to have Dorene worried about how I would progress to a clear and fully functional mind. Or if I might be stuck where I was at and never fully regain a true chain of thought.

Delusion

The Military Man

I remember explaining to Dorene that I thought people had thought I served time in the military. She answered me that this was not the case. Was I sure they thought so? I didn't explain about the Military Man experience. Was too fresh in my mind yet. I just wanted to make sure it wasn't put in my obituary. I see now why requests are made by the critically ill. Knowing their time is limited they want to leave this world on a clean slate. And a clear conscious.

I was attending a funeral for an old friend or family member on Dorene's side who was being buried in his uniform.

They basically just dug a hole to throw him in. Once the hole was dug, they rushed him out of the church after a brief service on a handheld canvas stretcher, like you would see in a war movie, and just tossed him in the hole. No casket. No grave side service and no salute.

I was appalled! It made me physically sick! Upon rushing him to the hole he lost his Garrison Cap. I rescued it from the wet ground as it had been raining. I tried to catch the people to reunite the beret with him, but they were too quick to throw dirt over him.

As I sat on a bench with his Garrison Cap in my hands and upset at what I had witnessed, people strolled by thanking me for my service, not knowing that the Garrison Cap didn't belong to me. So, at this point I felt I needed to clarify it with Dorene. To let people know I had never been in the military. She asked if I thought people thought I had been in the military and I said yes, there were some- only to realize these people were just a part of my delusion.

I have a nagging desire to stop at the Church and investigate the area dug up in my delusion. I wanted to just see if it is an actual grave site or empty space. After all, we drive by frequently on the way to the farm and it catches my eye every time.

I am hesitant simply because it's such a bad memory that revisiting it would be difficult.

We made the trip in the Fall of 2022. I finally got the courage up to walk the area in the cemetery and stand in the area where I witnessed the unthinkable act.

Standing near the exit of the Church, I was able to catch the same view as in my delusion. I could pinpoint the spot where I saw the mound of dirt and where the military man was deposited.

I walked from the Church to the spot where the hole was dug. The third row in from the parking lot and behind the second row of head stones. It looked remarkably like how it was in my delusion. Even the color of the headstones was the same.

As we looked the area over and began to recognize names on the stones (this has been the Abels family cemetery for over a century). Dorene pointed out that the area from my dream was the grave of someone we had known. He was a close friend of Dorene's family and a WWII Veteran. I had met him a couple of times but by no means knew him.

I've heard stories of his differences with the Church and its Pastor but not I'm not going to share them here.

I understand he went into the military in 1941 and spent much of his time in Guam and the Philippines. Dorene's father Gary mentions stories he would tell of the horrific things he witnessed while there and didn't talk of them easily.

I am in no way insinuating that the terrible treatment I witnessed in my delusion was how he was treated at his internment or that it was him at all. Just acknowledging the coincidence of his burial spot with the Military Man.

Pictured here is the church where everything took place in my delusion along with a picture of Sam, the family friend buried there. Sam very much matches the man in my dream. I should note when I met Sam he was elderly and I wouldn't have recognized him again if passing him on the street let alone as a young man like we see here. So, it is a bit disturbing to me that he resembles the Military Man so much.

Later, as I reflected on this delusion with my daughter, Erin, she had a revelation that gave me a new perspective. She said to me, "I think I know what your Military Man dream means. It represents your old body. There's a term in Christianity called being 'Born Again.' This means you die to yourself so you can live eternally with God/Jesus/Holy Spirit. In your former body, you were a soldier. You fought for your life. HARD. That person you were before all of this is dead and buried, and you are a new creation in Christ Jesus. Your picking up the beret makes me think you are still grappling with who you were before vs. who you have become. You are now a new man, and all guilt, sadness, etc. can no longer attach themselves to you. God has made you a new person in His image. Because He loves you."

I had to absorb this for a while. It makes sense.

Delusion

The Bathtub

When I came out of the coma, I was very confused. I wasn't sure where I was or why I was there. As many as 8 machines hooked up to me, I knew it was a dire situation. I was having trouble differentiating between reality and what was figments of my imagination, I was still keeping an eye out for the Killing Nurse as well.

I felt the need to bathe. I got out of my bed and undressed. I walked a little way coming up on what appeared to be a locker room with a large, tiled bathtub. Once I got near the tub my legs stopped working and I fell into the tub. Unable to move I began to yell out for help. Quickly 2 people came to my aid. One was a tall, slender young man with longish blonde hair pulled up and tied back nurse dressed in white and the other person was my brother Tom. Tom yelled at me "What the hell are you doing?". I was confused that Tom was there since he lives in Nevada, but it was nice seeing a familiar face.

They managed to lift me out of the tub and dress me. They then got me back into bed where I fell asleep. I'm still not sure what spurred this particular delusion. Maybe I was getting a sponge bath and was just reacting to that.

Delusion

Haley Working in ICU

One of the tricks my mind was playing was seeing my daughter Haley working in the ICU as an office clerk. I had seen her pass by several times. I finally got her to pop in briefly and asked her if she quit her job in Rockford to work here. Her explanation was The Thief (I never heard her real name) offered her the position for a lot more money and she couldn't turn it down.

I later saw her through my glass door working at a computer. She looked over at me and I smiled and waved. She was in tears. She yelled over to me "she (The Thief) snuck up behind me and cut my hair off". Haley had long wavey beautiful hair. I cried along with her and though I didn't think it was possible I hated The Thief even more.

Delusion

Crumpled Picture

In a dazed and confused state there was a nurse sitting along the side of my bed and I was lying on my side facing away from her. She must have been checking on my bed sore on my tailbone is the only reason I could come up with.

She produced a picture of me and Dorene. One like the old polaroid pictures on a hard plastic like paper. She said "Hey, look at this". I was feeling abandoned at this point trying to wake up and think clearly and in need of help but nobody from home was there. I was upset. I also couldn't speak so my actions had to speak for me.

I took the picture from her, crumpled it up and threw it back to her. She said, "But it's such a beautiful picture, did you look at it?" She handed it back to me and it was in perfect condition. I once again crumpled it up even smaller and threw it. In midair it straightened itself out and circled back to me. I did this several times. Each time I took a longer look at the picture. It was a very nice picture of us. I felt a sense of calm. I realized later that it was a delusion because I didn't have the use of my hands. Being comatose for so long my hands became frozen and had terrible pain from neuropathy. Pain, I found that would be with me for a very long time. Nerves grow back very slowly, and they had suffered a lot of damage. This would not allow my hands to have crumpled the photograph.

I believe the delusion was a way to tell me that Dorene was always with me and wouldn't leave me. When I did wake up enough to at least recognize people and get some understanding of what was going on, Dorene was there. Never so happy to see her in my life. Things were going to get better. At least for the moment.

The same nurse later commented on the pictures that were posted around my room and pointed out a particular photo of a cat and commenting that the cat seemed to be very comfortable and relaxed. I hated the thought of having to tell her the cat was actually dead. So, I kept it to myself.

Naturally there was nothing wrong with the cat in real life, but my mind kept thinking it had died.

September 2021

The first week in September 2021 my mind was clearing up. I was becoming more aware of my surroundings and situation.

I woke one morning to who I believed to be 2 doctors discussing my situation. One doctor was explaining to the other how if something continued, I wouldn't be a candidate. Not hearing the entire conversation, I assumed they were discussing a lung transplant. This is something I was not in favor of for many reasons. First being I was sure from the appearance of my surroundings I was in no way going to survive such an operation plus being diabetic and 62 years old were factors. Somewhat aware of my situation and how my body felt I knew there wasn't any way I would be able to survive such an invasive surgery.

Later discussions with Dorene would confirm my assumption that though briefly, it was a topic of discussion.

Coughing has been an ongoing issue. I cough constantly. The nurses tell me it's good that I cough and ask me if anything is coming up, what color it is and that I'm clearing my lungs. Also, having a trach, my coughs are weak and rarely productive. To try to clear the secretions blocking my upper airway, a vacuum hose is inserted into the trach and slid down into the windpipe to suction the mucous. I hate when they have to do this because it momentarily blocks my air and I can't breathe at all, makes me gag and is pretty aggressive. But once it's done, breathing is so much better it almost makes it worth what you went through! Obviously, it is worth it, but that doesn't mean I don't postpone it as long as possible. (I would continue to have to have this done until my trach was removed at Select Hospital.)

On ECMO I was informed that survival rate was low once it was removed. Many don't survive too long after being removed. This brought everything in my life into perspective. After fighting my way back this far only to die after waking up weighed heavy on my heart.

My biggest concern was how Dorene would take it. I wanted her to know life goes on. She should experience everything life has to offer. It doesn't stop just because I'm gone.

There was an ECMO Tech named Dave who occasionally looked in on me. I enjoyed his company. He looked to be about my age and could probably pass as someone in my family. Semi-retired he had a relaxed demeanor to him that put me at ease. I looked forward to having those relaxed conversations. It was a break from a mind that was cluttered and filled with worry.

Kelsey also played such a big part in my recovery. Very respected throughout the ICU. Many would say they spent time learning under her. I have a saying "You train animals and teach people". She was a teacher. And seemed to be highly respected, they said she was an outstanding teacher. She even brought me in a fidget spinner to help with dexterity with my hands. Her daughter gave it to her to give to me. She thought I could use it more than she would. How special is that? And that Kelsey would actually share my story with her family. Kelsey was the nurse that removed my restraints. I remember her asking me if I understood why I was being restrained. I said yes. I really wasn't sure why I was restrained other than in my delusions trying to strike out or escape. She said there won't be any problems if I remove them will there? I said no. She slowly removed them, and it was a wonderful feeling. My right wrist was first, and I quickly pulled it up to rub it with my left hand and I think it startled her. She slowly leaned back watching my reaction. Maybe she was aware of the Peter incident.

She and I had an understanding. If we respected each other then life would be the best we could make it. I grew to really like her. She was real, not fabricating emotion to try and cheer me up but was completely honest with me on where we were at with my situation. I appreciated how she dealt with me. She too, was another of my ICU Angels.

RENEWED VOWS

So, I suggested to Dorene that we renew our vows. This was something I have always been opposed to. Our original vows said, "Till Death do you Part," but I felt this could be a new beginning. A rebirth of our lives together. However short or long this time might be.

On September 7, 2021, we did just that. The ICU unit along with the ECMO people helped arrange everything including the WebEx with our family.

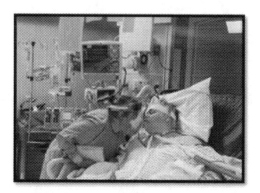

Our Daughter Haley sang, and Joshua our Son-in-Law performed the ceremony. They did a beautiful job. I found it very emotional and moving.

This reaffirmed my love for Dorene and gave me the opportunity to share my thoughts with everyone. Knowing my chances of surviving were low I wanted everyone to know how I felt.

I explained to Dorene that her life will go on. To experience all it has to offer and to not listen to any outside noise from people that might be negative. She deserves to lead a happy life and do all the things she had dreamt of doing. I don't think she was ready to hear this as she kept her face buried in my shoulder.

I then addressed the family to make sure they understood what I had just said and that they will support Dorene in anything she decides to do. That there was no reason she should not experience life to the fullest. I asked if they understood what I was saying, and they all responded yes.

Joshua then pronounced us Man and Wife. Through face masks and a face shield we kissed. It still had as much meaning to me as our original kiss nearly 39 years earlier. I felt at that moment I was confident the family would look after Dorene. I had come to grips with the fact I would not likely make the holidays and if that was God's decision then I was ok with this.

Everyone signed off WebEx and the crowd outside the big window of my room dispersed. I briefly saw Dorene's parents head toward the elevator. I commented to Dorene it was nice seeing them attend. I was told later that they had not attended, and they wouldn't have been allowed on the floor in any manner.

Dorene and Haley let me know they weren't confident my mind had been clear until weeks after I would get home.

As my mind cleared and my mental state stabilized, I was gradually given information on the events of the summer. Most of these events were very sad so they were gradually given to me, so I had time to process each one. There were times I had to tell Dorene no more for a while. She understood. The loss of so many friends and family were becoming more than I could handle.

We did discuss Erin's stay at St. Mary's in Madison and SSM Monroe for 2 months. She went very close to the same route as me being flown to Madison via MedVac. Intubated and in critical condition. She has her own story, so I won't go into it too much.

Apparently, this was 3 days before I went to the ER in Freeport. Apparently, we also had family WebEx meetings with doctors on how we wanted to handle her situation. While Dorene was explaining this to me, I realized I had no recollection of any of this. This put me in a state of shock. My first child nearly died, and I didn't know it. I felt the need to contact her right away and apologize for not being there and supportive until now.

I was also informed Erin's husband Joshua was admitted to the ICU with Covid and blood clots in his lungs. He fought hard not to be intubated and ended up getting through on a bi-pap machine and VapoTherm, eventually getting home after nearly a month, and being on oxygen. He was fortunately the first one to recover enough to get to visit Erin.

We would eventually be known to our family as - "The Miracle Three".

Erin made me feel better by saying she understood knowing I wouldn't remember due to my coma. But knowing she was only 8 minutes from me gave her comfort. She always knows the right things to say.

Once she was discharged from SSM Health Monroe, she managed to get to UW and visit me. She has a story to tell about this as does Haley our middle child. Again, I don't remember any visits during this period. I was still suffering delusions but apparently able to understand some things being told to me. I wasn't the best conversationalist I hear. Angered easily. They will delve into this deeper later in the book.

We would resume these conversations once I was settled in at Select.

While in ICU after waking up, Dorene brought in barber tools where she and Nurse Megan worked on me, trimming my beard, and cutting my hair. I was having trouble hearing and it was discovered the hair in my ears was so long Dorene said it could be braided. This was so thick in my ears it was hampering my hearing.

Megan regularly went above and beyond to try and make my situation as tolerable as possible. Next to Dorene she was the one who kept me the most motivated. She understood my loneliness for home and did everything she could to make my time there as positive as possible. She shared in my collapses as well as my victories. We laughed and cried together. She didn't have to go to these lengths for me, but she did. She is one of the most incredible people I have ever had the opportunity and privilege to meet and deserves as much credit as anyone with my survival. I can't express enough how much she means to me. Having never been in a situation like this I had no idea how to make it through it. Megan got me through it. I remember Megan having a span of 5 days in a row off and me being worried her being gone so long. It was a long 5 days. So happy to see her return.

I received many compliments when my grooming was all done, and I felt so much better also.

I had started physical and occupational therapy by this point and had made good progress. They were very good and understanding of my situation. The good days outnumbered the bad, and I feel very fortunate to say I beat the odds again. I was removed from ECMO, and my body responded very well. I spent 92 days in ICU setting a record and a record for time on ECMO of I believe 83 days.

Removed ECMO. It was a crazy procedure. I wasn't completely aware of my surroundings but followed most of it as it was going on.

A male doctor removed the line from my neck and applied pressure. A nurse took his place to hold it, eventually putting a large surgical bandage on it.

The doctor then moved to the line in my groin and quickly removed it, applying pressure. He motioned for the nurse (I believe Stephanie) to take over applying pressure and was told to hold it for 5 minutes.

Stephanie continued to apply pressure, checking periodically, but it continued to bleed. She summoned the doctor who ultimately placed a sandbag on the site to keep continuous pressure there for a prolonged period.

The doctor would later reflect that a couple stitches may have been warranted in this case, although that is not normal procedure. Maybe he didn't take into account how much longer the line had been in compared to the normal timeframes of other patients.

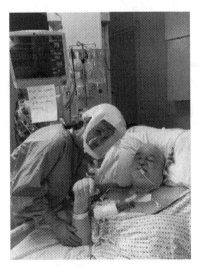

Cindy my PT pushed me. She is very special. Katie my OT did the same.

I had been craving water since waking up. In order to get to drink it

I had to pass a swallow test. This requires a camera on a cable run into your nose, down to your throat. They then record the different forms of liquid being swallowed.

The lady came in with all the different liquids for the test. I noticed Diet Coke in her tray first off. I was excited.

I was lying in my bed with the head of the bed raised slightly for looking out the window. She explained how the test would be done and inserted the camera in my nose. I explained to her I needed help sitting up and getting in a full sitting position. She told me we were going to do it like in the real world, right where I was. This made no sense to me. I never drink anything lying down.

She began with things like pudding and thicker stuff and that I managed to do ok. Then she got to water and Diet Coke which she had me sip from a spoon placed sideways to my lips and suck it from the spoon. This was impossible to do lying down and turned to the side like I was. When all the tests were done and she was preparing to leave she told me I had failed the thin liquid test and wouldn't be allowed water or Diet Coke. I was furious. I explained I failed because she didn't allow me to sit up. She continued to head towards the door, so I got even louder," So I'm supposed to just sit here and dry out?". She yelled back "I don't know what you want me to do." I yelled as she was going through the door, "Your job would be nice".

I made it very clear to everyone I spoke to after that about how it was handled and how upset I was not getting water or ice chips. My body felt the need for water in a way I had never felt before. It was a type of panic. And I had never been a big water drinker before, but it was a priority for me now.

Once I got to general care, I was given the same test again properly and passed easily. I always had a fresh glass of ice water with me after that.

I remember that night after having ECMO removed Nurse Anna (another of my Angels) coming in and viewing results of tests since being removed from ECMO and her letting out a cheer. She made mention to me that this number was very good meaning I was responding to life without the machine very well. Her excitement was genuine and gave me a real good feeling going forward. I always enjoyed hearing the door slide open and hear "Hi Kevin, it's Anna".

Anna and Megan

I then was moved to intermediate care for just over a week before being moved to general care.

Still being labeled as a covid patient, I remained on the covid floor. Once a covid patient, always a covid patient, even though a test in ICU determined I was negative for the virus.

All together I would spend 102 days in Freeport and Madison hospitals. It seemed a lot longer especially once I was moved out of ICU because visitors weren't allowed on the covid floors. Having visitors is what kept me going, and it was taken away. One person referred to it as isolation rooms. And that is exactly what it was. My most depressive period of the whole hospital stay. I would spend all but 2 hours of my time over this week and a half in bed. Losing the little bit of progress I had made in ICU with my standing.

One of those 2 hours were spent in a cardiac chair. For those not familiar it is an oversized straight back chair on wheels with very little padding, and I don't believe designed for comfort as much as function. They were unable to secure me the recliner I requested so replaced it with this.

Since I had been bed ridden for so long, I was hoping to get an opportunity to sit up in a soft chair and enjoy some normalcy. Maybe even watch a little tv. 2 male nurses came in and put me in a large sling and lifted me out of bed. It didn't feel that secure, but I held on long enough to get to the chair. Once in the chair I explained it wasn't at all what I expected when I was told a recliner and it wasn't very comfortable. They explained their inability to secure the other chair and to try it out for a few minutes and left.

About 15 minutes into sitting in it I was in so much pain I began calling for them to get me back to my bed. I was told I would have to be in the chair for at least an hour. I explained I couldn't take it anymore and wanted back in my bed. They said they would see what they could do. They didn't return to put me back in bed until the hour had long expired. By then I was in tears from the pain. No apologies, no nothing. They came in, moved me back and said "there ya go". If I had been my old self, I would have taught them some respect. Knowing my time there would be short I elected to chalk it up to experience and let it be.

I received a brief visit from my ICU Physician's Assistant Janyne who was checking in on me. She is an extra special person. More than just a great PA.

Janyne, Me and Dorene

This would be the last visit I had from her and all I did was complain about how bad it was there and how unhappy I was instead of thanking her for taking special time to come see me. I should have shown her the respect she deserves. I hope someday to get the chance to apologize and tell her how much she means to me.

SELECT SPECIALTY HOSPITAL

9-30-2021

Funny, I don't remember my transfer from UW to Select. Dorene has told me I was 2 hours later that the time she was told to be there. It's like in my bed at UW then I appear in this hallway talking to a very excited gentleman at a standing computer. Very welcoming. I'm hoping his name comes to me. I wasn't on that floor but a few days. The room had a weird air-controlled bed and was dark. I'm not sure if it was nighttime or not. I had no recollection of making the trip. Maybe they gave me something to calm me down before the ride. I was nervous about leaving. Mostly anxious. I definitely wanted out to somewhere with a little more freedom and allows visitors.

From my notes

My first day at Select and my first physical therapy session. I stood with a walker and pivoted to a wheelchair and back 3 times. I believe this surprised the staff knowing the condition that I was in when I left UW.

I currently have little to no use of my left hand and the use of only 3 fingers on the right. They are all but frozen in place. This makes tasks not only difficult for me, but the staff has to help me open bottles and pop cans, peel open foil food containers and milk cartons. They would also cut any food up I needed because I couldn't properly hold a knife.

After a discussion about the weather, it was learned by the staff that I hadn't been outside for 102 days. It was in the 60s and sunny, so I was taken outside for about 20 minutes.

The sun was so warm and felt so good.

Kind of looking forward to what tomorrow has in store. I think they were surprised at how easily I stood, transferred to the wheelchair and back after being bedridden for so long.

For a hospital, the food here is very good. What a pleasant surprise. The people are very nice as well.

Today, however, was not without issues. I waited 55 minutes for a bed pan. Initially a nurse came in and I asked her for one. She looked in the cupboard and didn't see one. Apparently, Dorene took that one home with my stuff since it came from UW.

The nurse then left to get one, so I thought. Fifty-five minutes later, after pressing my call light and yelling at a closed door, someone finally popped in and saved me from what would have been a mess to clean up. I learned from there to proact so to not end up in this predicament again. I had them place a commode next to my bed shortly after that.

Apparently, there was a patient who fell out of bed and as an emergency everyone on the floor responded.

10-8-2021

It has now been just over a week since arriving at Select. As I look back over the past week, I have come to realize just how much they have done for me. When I arrived here, I was basically bed ridden. In this week I have learned to use a walker where I walked 68 feet, stand on my own and I have walked for the first time today unassisted. It was only 24 feet but walking none the less. I can swing my legs out of bed and to the floor and sit on the edge of the bed. I was not able to do these things before I got here.

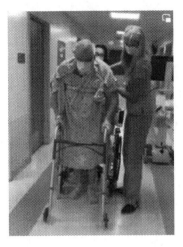

I have gone from a mask over my trach, to having a capped trach trial of 72 hours to ready me for its removal before going to Van Matre. They are limited to 6 liters of O2. It's their preference to not deal with traches. I will then be solely on the nose cannula.

Dorene reintroduced me to gifts from our old church from Pearl City Zion Community Church. A small handmade wooden cross that she had placed in my hand and prayed with me while I was at my sickest in ICU and a hand made blanket I would use until transferring to Van Matre. She says I have had them with me all this time, but I have no recollection of them. They are beautiful gifts.

The food is good. Not made like typical hospital food. Much made from scratch and like you may find in a restaurant or made at home. They have 6 talented cooks and a person who comes to you with an iPad to tell you the specials and take your order. A nice experience.

There have been a couple glitches with the staff, but they seem to correct and address issues quickly. All in all, it's a quality facility with awesome, knowledgeable people.

10-8-2021

Sitting here feeling sorry for myself, I can't help but look across the hall. I believe his name is Mike. He looks to be in the same shape I was in a couple of weeks ago, catheterized and bed ridden. He doesn't seem to get any visitors. How does a person get through all this stuff without having friends and family visiting? Dorene drove 2 hours each way, 2-3 times a week to visit me. Haley would ride with her. Ethan and Aurora, Erin and Josh also made the trips. All to make me feel loved and keep me positive in my rehab. It's what kept me pushing myself to get home.

I feel guilty taking so mush of Dorene's time. I know it's causing her to jump through hoops at work and at home. I don't deserve her but am so grateful I have her. I Couldn't have gotten this far without her. Hopefully I get to Van Matre next week to shorten that 2-hour drive to around 30 minutes.

It looks like Mike has contact with the outside world via a land line. We are all fortunate to have smart phones and the ability to use apps like FaceTime. Two to three times a day, I video chat with Dorene and Haley on days they don't visit. Dorene and I also FaceTime on her drive home so I can be sure she gets there safe. We also tucked each other in at night.

I feel I might be suffering from PTSD and survivor guilt. I'm crying all the time as my thoughts go to everything and everyone we have lost while I was asleep. Yet for some reason I was spared. So many people rallying behind me. It has become a little overwhelming.

I cry for those we lost, I cry thinking about going home, I cry about the thought of our whole family being able to celebrate Thanksgiving together. I cry when Dorene arrives and when she leaves. I cried when I used the walker for the first time and the same for when I took my first steps. This is a significant change of emotions for me. I could usually keep my emotions in check.

I watch the news and listen to people talk about how bad everything in the world is but my experience since waking up is completely the opposite. I see a world filled with faith, love, and support. I never knew there were so many out there that cared. What a wonderful world I live in. I never would have survived without their prayers and support.

I am currently in my first 24 hours of my 72-hour cap trial. This trial caps off my trach for 72 hours to force me to have to use a nose cannula. Once I reach the 72 hours and have no issues, they will remove my trach completely and 24 hours after that will meet the criteria to go to Van Matre. The last stop before home.

It's a scary thought. How will I cope? How will I control my O2 and medications? It will still beat being in the hospital.

Having visitors will help me get through the day. Ethan and Aurora will be stopping in. I haven't seen Aurora since before I got sick and even though Ethan visited me while I was in ICU I don't have any memory of the visits, so it's like getting to see him for the first time too. I'm excited not only for their visiting but that I can show them my progress. I know they were worried about me so I hope I can put them at ease. I'm not nearly as weak or ill as I was the last time Ethan was up to visit and I will actually be able to communicate some with them. Something I don't think from what I've been told I was able to do before. This will help me keep my mind from wandering to dark places. Ethan has always had a way of cheering me up.

I wonder if I should seek professional help for my PTSD? I don't enjoy my mind wandering and crying all the time. This isn't like me.

It's 9:30pm. This is the time I usually begin to feel anxious. My mind racing. Will I leave for Van Matre on time? Will I sleep tonight? Seeing going home soon. Not to mention revisiting the horrible delusions.

Trach will come out Monday morning. Looking forward to this. Can't wait to hear my real voice again. Not through a valve in my trach and to cough normally.

Can't wait until Sunday. Dorene and Haley will be visiting. Will be the first time I've seen Haley since I got sick. I can't wait! Tomorrow (Saturday) will be a long day of anticipation.

10-9-2021

Dreamt Dorene and I were newlyweds. She was wearing a red jumper short with white flowers and barefoot. We slow danced in the park with no music. People were slowing down as they passed by. All smiling with approval. What a nice change from all the bad things I had been experiencing to this point.

An eventful night. First Respiratory Therapist Brenda came to me at 9:00 pm saying I was having a sleep study. Where they were going to turn my O2 off while I slept to see how I would do on room air. Needless to say, I have a problem with this. I made it clear they weren't turning my O2 off and risking me not getting my trach out.

Brenda went back to her notes and read that I could do the test at 5 liters of O2.

10-10-2021

Now at 8:30 am I received word that I had passed the test. Another hurdle cleared.

Today my nurse is Maybelle. My favorite nurse. Dorene will also be visiting. It's going to be a good day.

Haley won't be visiting, however. She is struggling with a lung infection and is too sick to make the trip. And since it's a lung issue it makes it especially risky for me.

Currently waiting on breakfast. I am hungry. Heard over the pager that third floor trays have arrived.

Dorene arrived and helped me wash up. So much better having her here to help me with this after so long being washed up by nurses. Dorene worked on my face which was covered with dermatitis. One thing I wish we would have done better was take better care of my skin. After waking up and moving to intermediate care I noticed my skin was very irritated especially on my face. I pulled off cakes of skin from my ears and earlobes revealing dermatitis which was also thick around my nose and in my beard.

It was a mess. My skin was peeling off. It felt so much better once she was done. I can't wait to take a proper shower. I hear Van Matre will give me this opportunity.

10-11-2021

Feeling anxious. Pulmonary doctor was in at 3:00 pm. She gave the approval for the removal of my trach. Waiting for the RT to come in to do so.

Apparently, the insurance company requires the notes for the last 24 hours before they act. Doesn't look like my notes will make it on today's submission. I'm hoping this doesn't interfere with my transferring to Van Matre.

I have done everything asked of me and beyond. I'm hopeful this is enough to get me transferred by Wednesday.

It's now 3:30pm. Still hoping it comes out today.

On a lighter note, I was able to walk unassisted in the halls today. Much further than the last time. Twenty-eight feet, 68 feet, and 60 feet. Hope this improvement continues.

It's 4:30 pm and my trach is out! Unable to talk without holding my stoma closed. They don't stitch them closed; they allow it to heal naturally. Should be closed within 72 hours however my consistent coughing could extend it. I didn't feel it come out. Having been in so long I expect healing to take a while.

They've put a bandage over the stoma, and it feels weird because it does leak a little bit when I breathe or cough. All good though. I can talk a little if I put pressure on the bandage.

10-15-2021

I just had my discharge interview. Recounting my stay came to be emotional. We discussed my rapid improvement and how I surprised everyone. I didn't realize how many were stunned how quickly I was able to walk and how I managed to keep so much strength considering how long I was in bed.

Emily and Kahla, my OT and PT Angels, didn't cut me much slack through my time here. I was pushed some days to my limit. Something I enjoyed. No settling for mediocrity. I wanted to exceed my best each day. Walking the halls was a highlight for me.

Well, my hopes have been dashed. Van Matre no longer has a bed available. Insurance didn't come through in time so now I wait the weekend. Four more days at least before I can go.

Sam, my case worker, was visibly upset having to break the news to me again. Dorene said she was in tears when she made the call to her. What a special person she is.

10-18-2021

Here I sit, still at Select. Nearly a week after I was supposed to go to Van Matre. Upset over this, Dorene, and I, along with our case manager Sam, decided that if I didn't have a transfer by the next day I will be discharged to home. All my physical and occupational therapists agreed I was capable of handling being in a home environment. Though they thought the additional therapy that Van Matre would be best.

So now we plan for the worst-case scenario.

Dorene puts everything in motion preparing the house for my potential early arrival. Completed the ramp, getting O2 delivered along with an oxygen concentrator.

I'm torn between which plan I want to play out. I wouldn't mind going home, I miss it so much. But I also know that my physical therapy will take much longer than if I go to Van Matre. The additional therapy would make me feel more confident when getting home.

I have a way to go with improving my stamina and reducing my O2 liters. Guess we will see what tomorrow brings. I am satisfied either way. I just need to move on from here. I have accomplished everything I set out to here.

10-19-2021

I prefer my door being closed because of all the commotion in the hall especially during shift change at 7am. I hear nurses talking to CNA's and even other patients. One lady just keeps repeating "hello "for long periods of time.

This morning my door was left open. Through all the noise the morning brings I hear a familiar sound pierce through it all. It was a pill crusher. I remember all too well that sound in ICU as the nurses crushed my pills and inject them into my feeding tube. It was a good day when the feeding tube was removed. A good day here at Select when Maybelle my favorite nurse at Select removed my pic line. Never felt anything. She talked to me the whole time distracting me from what she was doing, then just held the line up so I could see it was out. Another step closer to normalcy.

Received notice I will be leaving for Van Matre at 4:00pm. Was hoping to go home but I know deep down that the additional therapy will do me good. My transfer date for Van Matre has been put off so many times I don't believe anything they tell me anymore.

Select has turned out to be a blessing as I look back at my time here. I was bed ridden when I arrived and now able to walk short distances when supervised. That's huge for someone who hasn't for almost 4 months.

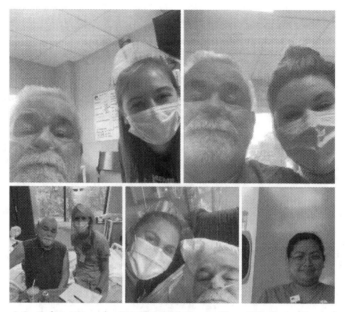

My Select Angels, Emily OT, Sam-Case Worker, Kayla PT, Jessica RT and Maybelle-My favorite nurse.

I did in fact leave for Van Matre at 5:00pm. Time to start my final chapter before going home.

Van Matre had me scared a bit. I thought for sure they were going to find something wrong with me that couldn't be fixed. Envisioned it being strict like a prison with hard therapy and in your room 21 hours a day.

It is my last stop before going home so I don't really care if it's scary or not. It's between me and home.

VAN MATRE ENCOMPASS HEALTH REHABILITATION HOSPITAL

I am nervous. I hear the therapy here is 3 hours a day and intense. I hope I am up to the task. With all I have worked towards I can't fail now. God give me the strength to succeed.

Sam, the Case Worker from Select, needs to be given some recognition. Her relentless work towards getting me to Van Matre puts her on my Angel list. I know it was emotionally draining on her with all the delays. She knew and witnessed my emotional collapse during these delays. She cried along with me.

Again, I am fortunate that through this journey I have had these very special people become a valued part of my recovery. These Angels looked after me. What would have happened to me without them? Where would I be?

When I arrived here at Van Matre, I was warmly welcomed by everyone I encountered. The people from Select Respiratory Therapies and University of Wisconsin at Madison TLC told me to expect intense therapy of 3 hours each day. This concerns me because I had only learned to stand and walk just a couple weeks prior.

My first evening Dorene was at my side as she has been throughout this long and difficult journey.

Once I got to my room and sat on my bed, the reality of understanding that this place was standing between me and getting home began to dawn on me. A bit overwhelmed, I began to cry. I asked Dorene while tears ran down my face if it was ok to be scared, because I was. Would I be able to pass the tests they put in front of me? Will they find something else wrong with me that nobody can fix?

Dorene in her own beautiful way explained to me that I had exceeded all expectations in every other challenge put in front of me to this point and this will be no different. "You got this, then home."

I decided then that I would be home in a week. I made this clear to doctors, nurses, my case manager, and physical and occupational therapists.

Dr. Knight said he appreciated my confidence, but normal stays are 2-3 weeks so not to get too overconfident should I be there longer than my plan. My response to Dr. Knight was "I will be home in a week." He just smirked a little, nodded his head, turned, and walked away with a nurse in tow.

10-20-2021

Well, day one is in the books. All indications are I did very well. Need to work on my hands quite a bit. Having been in the coma for so long my hands froze in a half-closed position.

My stamina is poor. Walking and exercise drop my O2 level quickly. Makes it difficult to reduce my O2 level down from 4 liters to 2 then eventually to none at all.

My back, legs and arms are sore but it's a good sore.

Meeting my new therapists, I am impressed in the condition they are in. Steve and Kamil are clearly athletes and clearly in very good shape.

10-21-2021

The day begins like all the others with visits from PT and OT. This morning we worked on getting clothes ready and taking a shower. Yes! My first shower since the middle of June. I have looked forward to this for such a long time. My only disappointment is the limited amount of time I will have. Breakfast will be here shortly and I'm hungry, and PT will start at 7:00am sharp.

The shower was amazing. Even though it was primarily in a shower chair, I was able to wash my hair with shampoo. I scrubbed and scrubbed my hair and was unable to get it back to being soft. The oil in my hair is so bad I can't stand it, and it might be some time before it returns to normal.

But I feel so good being this clean. A bit annoying having to have an OT there throughout the experience, but at least I was given privacy.

Once out of the shower and dressed mostly, I was given help with socks and shoes and making the bed. It was all very exhausting. I hadn't done this much on my own in a long time.

Had a nice breakfast of scrambled eggs, English muffin, and milk.

Steve then arrived to take me to physical therapy. He explained to me that when he just came in my room he had to take a look at the room number because he thought he might have entered the wrong room. He expected to see a person in bed and very challenged, not a person sitting on the edge of his bed writing in a journal. He was aware of my story and couldn't believe my recovery to this point.

We talked about my progress and what I wanted out of this. I explained I don't want to be treated as fragile. That I wanted to work hard and finish in a week. He agreed to work with me.

Their facility is well equipped. I look forward to trying many of these pieces of equipment out. Today though will be spent walking. It was difficult but I did walk farther than I had at Select. I walked twice with distances of 160 and 180 feet. It caused my O2 to drop significantly so we decided to take more breaks while walking instead of pushing so hard.

The schedule is 3-3 ½ hours a day. In increments of 1-1 ½ hours and as many as 3-4 scheduled times the schedule comes out the afternoon before. It switches back and forth from PT to OT. My day generally will start out with OT to get me dressed and ready for the day.

10-22-2021

Had a special visitor today. I finally got to see Haley for the first time since I became sick. At least that I can remember. As usual I cried when she arrived and again when she left. She also snuck me in some fast food.

That's my girl!

10-23-2021

Today is Saturday, a rest day from physical therapy. I initially wanted therapy all weekend but knowing I will be discharged Wednesday and how worn out I was I was happy to get the rest. Having not slept well and with soreness all over, rest was needed.

Today near the end of October I need 4 liters of O2 and lack stamina. It will be a long road to recovery yet but at least they are saying it will eventually come back to me along with the use of my hands. Also, gradual relief from the neuropathy. Guess I just need to be patient.

10-25-2021

We have been working with all the equipment lately. I walked steps for the first time. Up and down 3 steps. Difficult but I did it. Also used the arm bike and then both arms and legs. They also have a mockup of a car to get in and out of. I found getting in and out of it wasn't as easy as it looks.

At first, I just thought I would jump in like I normally would and failed miserably. My legs weren't strong enough to hop into the car. I almost fell to the floor. Catching myself on the way down. Kamil them showed me the proper way to enter and exit the car. I was able to manager doing that!

10-26-2021

After completing the day's therapy and finishing what I had needed to be considered "graduated" and safe to be discharged, tomorrow I head for home.

Once you complete your time, your last task is to ring the bell. This lets everyone know you're going home. It was very emotional. It was the last task before home. I've waited so long for this. I can't believe tomorrow is the day!

As I sit in my room on my last night at Van Matre, I can't help looking out through my room door across the hall into an elderly woman's room. Her name is Karen. What's weird is I normally keep my door closed.

As I'm peering into Karen's room, and I see 2 Nurses enter her room with one Nurse on each side of her bed and I hear "So you need a boost?"

The hospitals I have been in refer to a boost when a patient has slid down in their bed and doesn't have the ability to adjust themselves. The 2 Nurses will grab ahold of the underneath sheet and pull the patient back up to the head of the bed.

It dawned on me that just 3 weeks before I was having my Nurses and CNA's doing the very same thing. Now I get in and out of bed on my own and even walk to the restroom. This may not seem like a big deal to most but after being bedridden for nearly 4 months it's huge.

I feel for those patients and their challenges. I know from my experience they aren't easy. Fortunately for at least the patients at Van Matre, they are receiving excellent help.

I have no idea what condition I would be in without the excellent care and therapy I have been privileged to receive from the people at Van Matre. Many others aren't so lucky.

You learn after experiencing my type of disability that pride and vanity are thrown out the window. Between bed pans and sponge baths you learn to accept the situation you are in.

The Nurses and CNAs without complaint take care of all your needs. Cleaning you up after bowel movements to washing you up with sponge baths. Fortunately, once I got to Van Matre, I was self-sufficient with all my personal hygiene. It was also my first chance to take a nice, long, hot shower.

Today at Van Matre I also received a green wrist band. This signifies I can travel in my room as I please. Though I will only be here for another 15 hours or so, it is a feeling of success and accomplishment. Haven't had that freedom since getting sick. Helps build my confidence going forward.

I was admitted on a Tuesday evening. First full day was Wednesday. So here I sit on the following Tuesday night looking forward (1 week later as I predicted) to going home at 10:00am tomorrow.

It once again proves that Dorene had more confidence in me than I did myself. Like the other stops along the way I made the decision to exceed their expectations. I must have done this.

GETTING HOME

I left Van Matre on Wednesday October 27th. A day I never thought would come. There were times early on where I wavered in my confidence and tried to plan a message to leave for my loved ones that would try to explain how much they meant to me and hopefully have a little wisdom for them to carry with them too.

On the 26th of October, the day before discharge I completed my last therapy sessions. Upon leaving the gym area there is a bell the person rings that signifies they had completed their time in therapy. I got to ring that bell. Once I did, I heard a thunder of applause and yells congratulating me. Everyone lined up and wished me well as I was wheeled back to my room. I would later receive a card in the mail where everyone signed it with well wishes. It is very special to me. They were great personalities to get the best out of me.

On the 27th, my discharge day I participated in my interview. Mostly the same routine as previous stops except for my continued therapy. They initially set me up with FHN's Burchard Hills facility for continued rehab. I was not in favor of this. I have been there before, and they are very capable in their jobs, but it is also a community atmosphere that I didn't feel was in my best interest. So much as a cold could land me back in the hospital. After our discussion they agreed with me. They weren't overly familiar with the process there. We arranged in home therapy.

It was finally time. Time to drive home. Dorene was there and my PT's Steve and Kamil were both outside while getting me in the car. Dorene finally got to meet them.

It was a beautifully sunny day in the 60s. The drive home was a quiet one. Absorbing the beauty of the drive there was the occasional "We're going home" spoken through a broken and emotional voice. Words cannot explain properly how happy Dorene and I were. It could be felt in the car.

We finally reach our long driveway. As the house comes into view the first thing I see is this massive ramp that was built for me by Dorene's family. It is very impressive. I knew I would be able to manage getting in and out of the house with hopefully little effort for Dorene and myself.

The next thing I saw was all my kids waiting for me. This made me crack. They were there. What a wonderful surprise. Just another gesture of their love. I looked to Dorene and said, "we're home." She responded, "yes we are." All the anticipation and concern on how I was going to function at home melted away. I knew I had people to lean on should I need them.

I opened my car door and gradually got my weak legs out to sit on the side of my seat while Dorene managed my O2 and pulled the wheelchair out from the back of the car.

Ethan, my son, readies the wheelchair for me and I slowly walk the few feet to it and sit. Ethan begins backing me up the ramp to the front door. Unable to fit through the door due to a screen door bracket Ethan goes for the tools to remove it. This gives me the time to absorb everything going on around me. I'm about to go into my home for the first time in 4 ½ months. What a feeling it is. All our pets came out to greet me. Tank was especially happy.

Ethan gets me through the door and into the house. I leave the wheelchair in the kitchen and begin walking towards my chair in the living room. Something I really missed along with my bed.

I sit down in my chair and release an audible sigh. I sink into the comfort of my chair.

I hear Aurora (Ethan's fiancé') make the statement "I feel the energy back in this house, it isn't so sad anymore." This was such a nice feeling. Everyone seemed to be happy. We were all home again.

We celebrated with Chicago style deep dish pizza. A big change from my meals being portion controlled and carb friendly that I had become accustomed to in the hospitals. You could say my diet over the first few days weren't following any diet a diabetic like me should indulge in. My stomach was a mess for a week. My system was not prepared for it. I have gone back to counting carbs and portion control. My body seems to appreciate the decision.

It's now 3 weeks post getting home. The challenges are many. It's much more difficult than I thought it would be. I wonder every day if I didn't leave Van Matre too early and take an additional week to build my stamina.

Having placed chairs in specific areas along the routes I would be frequently using became an important part of my safety. Each trip is an adventure. Sometimes I make it to my destination before having to sit and sometimes I don't and have to sit earlier.

I am fortunate that Dorene has been able to take 2 weeks off and spend it with me and help me learn how to get around. I appreciate the supervision.

My Mother, God rest her soul, shared a story with me about my Father who passed away from cancer back in 1978. The story goes like this. My Father became ill and was admitted to the VA Hospital in Long Beach California. My parents live in Ontario California about an hour and a half away. After a lengthy stay my mother was told that he would be coming home, and oxygen will be delivered, and he would return home the following day.

The oxygen was delivered on a Tuesday. My Mother prepared for his arrival. During my father's time while living in Ontario he has this thing about having the tv on 24 hours a day. Much of the time sleeping in front of it on the couch especially once he became sick. Late that Tuesday night or early Wednesday morning my mother got up from bed, wandered to the living room and turned the tv off. She didn't know what prompted her to do this, but it is something she regretted the rest of her life.

My Father passed away at precisely the same time as the tv getting turned off leaving my mother wondering if it was due to her actions. She received the call about my father's passing a short time later. She explained to the caller that it had to have been a mistake that he was supposed to come home in the morning. They assured her there was no mistake leaving her stunned and with a feeling of guilt. I tried my best to convince her that her actions couldn't have caused it and it was an act of God. It still makes a person wonder however how mom knew to turn the tv off. I do believe soul mates sense things about each other. Feel each other's sadness and pain. And you can never take God out of the equation.

I went to the ER on June 19th, 2021 and spent four and a half months fighting for my life and in physical therapy. During this time my wife Dorene knowing the story about my parents made a point in leaving the tv on. The tv would stay on until the night of me getting home with me being the one who turned it off.

She didn't share this with me until I had turned it off. She was pulling out all the stops. Anything to get an edge to get me home. And once again my eyes filled with tears, and I held her tight. What an amazing person I have.

One night I was having terrible lower back and hip pain that ran down my left leg. This led to a trip to the ER at FHN. The last thing I wanted to do was visit a hospital again but with my pain at an agonizing 10 I didn't have a choice.

In September 2013 I had a stimulator surgically put in my back. This was an internal computer next to my spine in my lower back with wires that run up the inside of my spine and connect to the nerves that control the feeling in my lower back.

The premise is when turning the stimulator on there is control over the degree of stimulation you want. Like a ten's unit but far more intense. You can crank it up to the point the stimulation covers up the pain, eventually relieving your pain.

When the unit failed to cover up the pain, I realized the problem I was having was something other than the nerve pain I had suffered in the past.

I do not recall doing anything to my hip that would cause an injury. I did drive my roadster that is a manual, which may have contributed to the issue. It was sore after driving it. It was only 5 or 6 miles, but I did go through the gears quickly. Having Ethan help me back out of the car I felt some soreness. It went away for a couple days, but then came back with a vengeance.

Dorene took me to the ER where I was taken in quickly. The people there were genuinely nice. The doctor seemed very capable. A pleasant change from the ER there I had seen in the past.

To give me some quick relief I was given morphine and oxycodone.

This did help take it down to a level that was tolerable so they could get me to the X-ray room.

The x ray showed an inflammation in the hip (osteoporosis and arthritis) causing irritation. I was given pain meds to take home and told to follow up with my primary physician. This is what I did.

My primary agreed with the ER doctor. We agreed to put off therapy for a week or 2 and I'm to follow up after a week to see if there is any progress or if we need a different approach.

The use of steroids along with a muscle relaxer and oxycodone has helped some but pain at night is still enough to keep me awake.

The following day I continued to have pain. I spent the day stretching, in pain and uncomfortable. It let up some before bed, so I thought maybe everything I had done during the day was paying off. I was wrong. At 3:00 am I was woken with a great deal of pain.

Rather than wake Dorene with my tossing and turning I decided to go to the living room and try to get comfortable in my recliner.

Having trouble there as well I tossed from side to side.

As I stretched out in the chair, I slid off the chair to the floor. I wasn't concerned at first. How hard could it be? I struggled for about 10 minutes and was unable to get off the floor. I was forced to call to Dorene for help. Hated waking her up.

She tried to get me up to a chair, but I was too heavy and very little help. I noticed my left leg was much weaker than my right. I didn't notice this when standing or walking.

It was time for reinforcements. Dorene went upstairs and got Haley, our daughter, up to help. With one on each side, they were able to get me to a chair. I honestly didn't realize how bad the deconditioning was in my legs and arms.

They made the decision right then to get me an Apple Watch should I fall with nobody home. This would prove to be a good decision later.

The steroids did however help me some with my hands. I can now close my right hand and the thumb; index finger and middle finger feel almost normal with swelling and neuropathy still in the other 2 fingers.

My left hand can close about ¾ of the way to a fist. This is from only being able to bend my fingers slightly. If the hip pain continues, I will be forced back to my doctor to get an CT Scan and see if anything is torn. Not looking forward to that. I'm unable to have an MRI due to the stimulator in my back.

Another realization is my clothing. For the first time today, I decided to wear jeans instead of the sweatpants I have been wearing since being at Select.

At one point just after I woke up in ICU, I was down over fifty pounds. Some doctors said my muscle mass played a big part in my survival. It was also another thing that Covid took from me. My pants fall off me. My shirts are loose as well. I have put some weight back on once the feeding tube was taken out, but I am still down 35 pounds or so and my muscle mass is all but gone. They say for what I have been through I'm very strong but far away from where I was before getting sick.

So, recovery continues.

Now that Dorene is back to work, I only see her at lunch time for about a half an hour. This gives me alone time to write and try to help with daily chores to take some of the burden off her. I don't do much yet but improving a little bit each day.

It also unfortunately gives my mind a chance to wander. Some call it PTSD, I guess. It is no picnic. I do not know everything about what happened while I was asleep, but I know enough about what my family had to go through to convince them to let me live.

It is too difficult for me at this point to listen to everything that happened, and I have asked Dorene to document everything and put her spin on the days I was asleep.

I think about a good friend of mine who lost his battle over the Summer just 2 weeks after he texted Dorene to check on how I was. How my nephew Brian and my brother Bobby participated in the discussions and fought along with the family.

How the administration told them and my kids they could not have an open mind on what I would really want. This did not go over well. How passionate they were, fighting for me. The difficult positions I put them in and the emotional toll it must have taken on them. I hate the thought of putting them through all of this. I just sit and weep. A lot. Why was I spared? Everything now has a more profound effect on me. When my kids visit and when they leave especially.

I have not seen other family members yet as we are keeping me protected from the outside, but I have made a point of being in contact with them via FaceTime and texting. These conversations I hold dear to my heart. I find myself going back and rereading them. Each conversation fits their piece into the puzzle of my story. Each one leaving me in tears of disbelief the lengths they went through.

Sometimes I just cry from the fact I am sitting here at all. While in the ICU I really did not expect I would be going home. With garden hose-sized tubes running into my neck and out my leg along with being on a ventilator, the situation seemed insurmountable. I told myself I would fight until the end, whenever that might be. Every visit I had with Dorene I thought could be my last, so I put extra pressure on her to visit. I'm not proud of this as I look back. Putting this added pressure on her. But if I woke up in the morning, I considered it a victory and one more day I am a part of the living. Also 1 more opportunity to see Dorene. One more visit from her each day was what I was living for.

We are sitting here in our living room and the phone rings. It is our son in law Joshua telling us that his car was ready to be picked up and could Dorene take him. This is a matter of replacing the hoses and being told it would be four hundred dollars. They knew their situation with Erin being disabled from Covid and just did a patch job to make it drivable and cheaper. This is another thing that weighs on me. I would usually do these things for them and save them the money. No different with the things that need to be done around here. It is so frustrating thinking so many things I could do before will have to wait until at least Spring or maybe even Summer before I would be capable of doing them.

To recover from this requires much more than just the physical conditioning. It requires a mental state that can accept the reality of the situation you are in. With everything I have gone through you would think I was in control, but I am not. Every day is a struggle. Every day presents a situation that tests me.

I'm just hoping the future allows me to regain enough of my old self to get back to being a productive member of this family. I miss being helpful to my family. Being retired gives me the opportunity to be helpful. I just need to get there.

Winter brings a whole host of issues along with it. With my muscle loss I need to be especially careful while out in the cold. Especially with my hands. My circulation is poor, and they sometimes turn blue while in the house. Doctor says they are still healing from the inactivity and to be extra careful when going out into the cold. To wear gloves and bundle up extra warm when going out. I can already feel the cold's effect on me just when taking the dogs out. I never cared for the cold, but I could tolerate it. I guess it will be another trial-and-error situation.

Today is November 24th, 2021. The day before Thanksgiving. There is so much to be thankful for and so happy I get to spend it with my family. The Family was having a large gathering at the farm. This was something Dorene and I weren't comfortable with, so I stayed home and spent time visiting with them over FaceTime.

11-28-2021

Today has been a very eventful day. I went to my first appointment with my pulmonologist. Upon arrival the receptionist apparently was reading the history of my time in the hospital, and I heard an "Oh My" before continuing our conversation. She said she was happy to see I was still with us. I was a miracle. Not the first time I had heard this.

Dorene wheeled me back to the waiting area where a nurse moved me into the room. The nurse was surprised as well after hearing and reading my story.

After answering the typical questions, she stepped out and said the doctor would be in shortly.

Dr. Q came in shortly after. This was our first time meeting him since this was the first time any of us needed this type of doctoring.

It started off again as your typical first appointment; "How are you feeling, can you walk, how many liters of 02 are you on?" Stuff like that. He then began asking the questions pertaining more to my hospital stay. He was reviewing my chart at this time and became more somber and silent the more he read. I heard a faint "wow." He asked about timeframes of hospitalizations. Don't think he was prepared for what he heard.

Dorene mentioned the 3 months on ECMO, and he slowly turned back to the computer screen and quietly stated that only 1 in 10 people survive this. I told him I had set the record for that hospital. His response was that God was the only reason I made it through this and that there was a purpose for this, and I needed to discover what this purpose was.

We then began to get down to business. He was frank with me about my recovery and that it would be a lengthy one. I appreciated this of him. Some look at me as fragile and to always try to paint a rosy picture. I would much rather hear it straight, so I know what I need to expect of myself as well as them.

Respiratory therapy 3 times a week at the hospital, x-rays, and regular tests on O2 levels while walking and activity. The preliminary test today showed exactly what I told them to expect. It didn't matter whether I was on 2 liters or 6 it was the same result. My O2 dropped into the low to mid 80s and would recover in about a minute at rest. So, I remain on 2 and have no O2 support sometimes at rest. I lately haven't been wearing it to bed and I seem to be fine.

Hopefully with this regiment I will be able to kick it sooner than later. Dr. Q seems to think I will.

Now November 26th, I put my Apple watch to use. There is a slight rise of about an inch and a half between the kitchen and the mud porch. This is the exit to the deck and the yard.

Our 2 dogs (Brutus and Tank)

Our dogs needed out to go potty. Something I have done many times since being home. I headed to the kitchen with the dogs and attempted the transition from the kitchen through the doorway to the mudroom and caught my right foot in the doorway. It was just the tip of my shoe that caught the rise in the doorway, but it was enough. I overcorrected a little bit and extended my right foot out in front of me. When my foot hit the floor in the mudroom it slid out in front of me. Not unlike falling on the ice.

My right leg sliding out in front of me with my left leg still behind me in the kitchen side of the doorway. Now falling backwards, I am sensing this is not going to be good. I have had several shoulder surgeries from falling like this and have a good idea on what to do to reduce the chance of injury. One thing is not to reach back or use your elbow to break your fall, so I kept them by my side and tried to slightly turn to my right. This would have been fine if I wasn't in a doorway.

I went to the floor hitting my elbow on the door jamb then striking it on the floor despite my efforts. My left leg bent back and stuck underneath me. All I could think about was I was in trouble and not sure if I had broken anything. I had already proven with the chair incident I would be unable to lift myself up to any chair. The closest chair was about 15 feet away anyways and I was stuck in the doorway.

Dorene was on the other side of town running errands and not expected to be home for a couple hours so when I texted her from my Apple watch I also texted my daughter Erin and her husband Joshua who are only a block and a half away. I got an immediate response from Erin saying Josh was on his way.

Feeling better knowing help was on the way I began to assess for injuries. My left leg was caught under me and was going to take some work getting it out and in front of me.

I rolled to my right side and felt immediate pain in my right elbow and my left knee. I managed to free my left leg and straighten it out. My knee was hurting but I could tell nothing was broken. This was a big relief, but my elbow was still hurting.

Josh arrives and gets me sitting up. Second assessment tells me I have fared pretty well. Knee is sore but ok.

Josh gets behind me and lifts me to a chair he placed behind me. Sitting on the chair I was sore but felt like I could manage walking back to my chair in the living room. I made it fine, and Josh took care of the dogs.

I did realize the situation with my legs was bigger than I thought. I felt good while standing which gave me a false sense of security. If there is an event that puts me on the floor I'm there until I can get help to arrive.

Anyone having these types of issues need a source of communication. My situation could have been much worse in a lot of ways. What if my leg had been broken or I had suffered a head injury? Home safety has always been a focus of ours, but these times are different from the past. Not just because of my issues but other things like our age and the current world we are dealing with, as well as Covid and its variants.

11-29-2021

There is a calendar wipe board in our kitchen where we have always posted different activities and appointments so we would all know who should be where at any given time. This has proven to be valuable tool.

This calendar has information from the summer and Dorene couldn't bring herself to erase it. I have made a point of not reading it just because I really didn't want to know. There are chairs set throughout the house for me to rest at going from point to point. One of these chairs is just a few feet from this calendar. on this chair I was drawn to the calendar and began studying it. I can see why Dorene couldn't erase it. It documents the family cookout before we all got sick, and life was carefree. Then how rapidly our world was turned upside down. First Erin, then Josh and me. A step by step and day by day of events through June 22. 4 days after the 22nd were struck out and then nothing. The world and time stopped. This was when Dorene, Haley and Ethan's time was absorbed by the unthinkable. They were potentially going to lose half of their family at one time.

The calendar has still not been erased. I have tried but can't. I can't stand looking at it now knowing what it says but can't erase it because of what it documents. As a Genealogist I must respect the history regardless of my own personal opinion

I have heard from people with their opinions on what to do with it. Everything from throw it away to erase it and move on. The best advice for me so far is from my OT Gretchen. Her advice was to get a duplicate calendar and mount it over top of the original. This helps with the moving on and protects the original for the future. I think this will be the route we take.

December 2021

Entering December, the thought of the holidays brings a whole host of concerns interfering with the planning of family gatherings again. Choices must be made on just how we plan on celebrating as a family.

Covid is raging in this area, and we can't be too cautious. Everyone understands the concerns and are willing to do whatever it takes to be able to be able to spend it together.

We have all now had our vaccinations and/or booster shots. Not sold on vaccinations with the cases skyrocketing even with the vaccinated. Still losing family and friends regularly, it's simply not the answer, nor enough to make us feel comfortable.

We have decided leading up to the holidays we will practice strict social distancing, wearing of masks and will take a rapid test 24 hours before gathering. We are hoping by practicing all these precautions it's as close to safe as we could get. One nice thing is that nobody complains. Everyone is all in. This is a family who believes being together on Christmas Day means more than any roadblock that could be thrown in front of them.

The Covid problem is the worst it has ever been in this area. No rooms in the hospitals. Sending people home when they clearly needed to be hospitalized simply because there are no rooms.

We still either have groceries delivered or picked up. Avoiding the public as much as we can. I lost another friend as recent as 2 days ago, keeping this all still so fresh in my mind.

Health-wise, much is the same. Some improvement in all areas. Still wearing an oxygen cannula and on 2 liters.

As I try to improve on my day-to-day activities and expand my household chores, I find I still struggle with stamina though my legs are slightly improving as the weeks have gone on.

I have a bubbler on my oxygen concentrator that requires filling about once a week. This had run out of water, and I could tell the air was dry so I thought I would remove the container and fill it while I was working in the kitchen and doing laundry. After filling the concentrator bubbler, I finished in the kitchen and switching the laundry and decided to head back to the living room since I was feeling the need to rest. I try to stand and stay upright for 20 minutes at a time to build stamina. Sometimes longer, sometimes less.

When I arrived at my chair in the living room, I felt especially tired for some reason and couldn't seem to catch my breath. It's not unusual for me to drop to an O2 level in the low to mid 80s but recover quickly, usually in a minute or 2. However I wasn't recovering and the longer I waited the worse I felt.

I finally did an O2 check to be sure I was in fact recovering. My O2 level was 67. Not good. I rested a few minutes and tried it again. It rose to 77. Still felt bad, maybe even a little worse. I'm now to the point I am beginning to panic. I pull my cannula off and hold it to my lips to feel for air. There isn't any. Now I am concerned because I am home alone and obviously in some distress.

I knew at this point I wouldn't be able to troubleshoot the concentrator or even walk to it. I tried texting Dorene at work but didn't get a response. I then called her. She answered and left work immediately. She arrived home and began troubleshooting the machine. I told her I had filled the bubbler and thought that might have something to do with it.

She pulled it apart and found that I had put the cap back on cross threaded. That along with me putting the bottle into the holder sideways facing away from the living room. This caused the hose to kink at the bubbler. Once she fixed the cap and turned the bottle to face me my air resumed. It would take some time for me to regain an acceptable and regular O2 level.

I am stunned at how this stupid little mistake could have turned into something severe. What do others do if they don't have a support network like I do? It makes a person become ultra-sensitive to their surroundings. It seems you must pay close attention to all your actions. Overly cautious for your safety. Is this any way to live? It's a necessity to make it through the day but nothing you are accustomed to. How do you still live your best life and go through it while still being aware of every step you take? I only hope this doesn't go on too long.

I'm not bitter, at least I don't think I am. I understand how fortunate I am getting to spend the holidays with my family when I know of so many who didn't get that chance. Should I be feeling this frustration or just be content with the situation I have? I personally think not being satisfied or unhappy with my situation is a positive thing. It forces me to not accept my current situation and fight to get through it.

Some say it's only been 3 months, give it time. But 3 months is a long time when you struggle every day. I don't know how disabled Veterans and others deal with it.

The first and biggest obstacle is my stamina. My lungs need to sustain a high enough O2 level while active thus giving me the endurance to walk further. This is the issue that bothers me the most. Am I going to get my full lung function back? Not likely. But I want it back enough at least to where I could walk in the park or around our property. Helping my son work on home improvement projects at his home.

Yeah, I'm angry. I'm frustrated, but I'm alive. For today at least that's good enough.

12-23-2021

Today was therapy day. Both physical and occupational.

Started off with physical therapy. Misty, my therapist, tested me on balance and turning tasks. These are areas I've had trouble with in the past. Surprisingly I did very well. So well in fact she told me I was safe in my home. Haven't heard that yet. We discussed where my strength was at. We agreed my leg and core strength was very good. Not what it used to be but good enough if my O2 level would stay up. Therein lies the problem. My legs and the rest of my body starts starving for oxygen quickly. Though I recover quickly my legs have a limited amount of time before they tire to the point I need to sit.

I knew the respiratory part would take the longest and be the most work to get back, but I really didn't think it would affect everything else like it does. It only makes sense it would when I think about it.

Christmas Day 2021

Christmas night was spent at our son Ethan's house with all our kids and special guests. Ethan presented me with a box set of the tv show Psych. My favorite show. He said knowing it was my favorite show it gave him comfort knowing this and made a point of watching the entire series while I was asleep. I said thank you for the gift and he said no, it's yours. I said, "so you're giving it to me"? He and Haley said "no, you were given this for Christmas last year or the year before". I told them I was confused; I don't remember having gotten this and I was sure I would have remembered. They assured me this was the case. I have many blank spaces in my memory. We joked we could just give me the same presents each year and I would still be surprised.

12-26-2021

The day after Christmas. A day that has significant meaning to me. While in the hospital during my confusion stage I was learning what my situation was. I sensed that my health was not good and that me seeing the holidays wasn't probably in my future. I had trouble accepting this as you could probably imagine, but I knew it was in God's hands from here.

I prayed to God to at least make it to Christmas. If not making an extra day beyond Christmas I wanted to spend Christmas with my family. I would later move my release date up to Thanksgiving and later to Halloween because of my progress but the day I prayed for was Christmas. A day our family have always cherished as a Family Day to be together. Today being the day after Christmas, I have to say I was very nervous all night. I had issues with my breathing all night. Each time I woke up in the night I was wondering if that was it. Was God calling me home after our "deal" had expired? I stayed close to Dorene all night but being careful not to wake her. I finally managed to fall asleep for a little while. I checked my O2 level right as I woke up still feeling short of breath. Running around 90 I thought that was low for being at rest and having my canula in place.

I pulled my hose towards me a foot at a time. It's a 50-foot hose so untangling it takes some time. I found several kinks in the hose and fixing them. This solved my oxygen issues and I'm breathing much better.

I won't take these days I've been given for granted. Let's face it, my furthest outlook was Christmas with my family. I have not planned anything beyond this point. I got up, got dressed and sat in my chair wondering just what I might do today.

I can't wait for 2022. Looking forward to putting 2021 behind us.

12-30-2021

2021 is winding down. These few days leading up to New Years have been challenging. Everything from continued O2 problems to the return of my trigeminal nerve pain. For those who aren't familiar this is when (in my case) the number 5 nerve that runs down the left side of my head from my forehead, down the side of my face to my chin. The nerve spasms causing a sensation I can only describe as a seizure. The pain in unlike anything I have ever experienced before. It has been some time since I have experienced this event and was hoping it was a thing of the past. Not the case.

The cause of this is mostly unknown. I believe it was from some poor dental work but don't know this for sure.

My O2 has caused A-fib like heart abnormalities. This due mostly from my inability to keep my nose cannula in place throughout the night. On one occasion my O2 had dropped to 62 causing my heart to race. I woke up at 3:30 am hearing a pounding noise. At first, I thought it was the neighbor pounding on his race car, but I realized it was my pulse pounding from my head into the pillow. I knew this wasn't normal, so I checked my heart rate, and it was 117. I sat up and decided to use the restroom once my O2 reached 90. My heart rate had jumped to 122 once reaching the restroom. I returned to bed and tucked myself in. It was now 107 so trending in the right direction.

I checked everything for the half hour following my return to bed and my vitals gradually returned to what I have learned to be normal for me. All I believe caused from my cannula coming out of my nose.

Physical therapy was challenging today. Mainly because I decided to challenge myself. Once I finished my normal regiment of cycling and exercise, I asked Misty what was next. She said I could pick something. My suggestion was squatting. Since Dorene was home, I felt safer should things not work out. I have had my problems in this area but felt my legs have gotten stronger lately and felt I was ready to try this again.

We went to the kitchen, and I placed my hands on the island. I did my squat and was unable to return to a standing position. Not only did I not stand back up, but it wasn't even close. I had nothing. Dorene and Misty lifted me back up to a standing position. We decided to use chairs to lower to. The first chair was a normal dining room chair. I managed this easily. We then went to a child height chair, and I struggled but was able to do it. It felt good to struggle and push myself. So much that while the three of us were talking I kept doing the squats. To the point my legs eventually turned to jelly.

I wobbled a little bit while standing and Misty moved in just in case, she had to catch me. She asked if I was messing with her because others tease her like that. I said that was good to know for the future, but no, I did in fact wobble. At that point we all thought it was time to take a break. Dorene and Misty helped me to my chair.

I was sore and tired and felt good. It was nice to push through and improve.

12-31-2021

Gretchen showed up for occupational therapy. Feeling sore from yesterday I was anxious as to how I would do. Other than the weak knees and a sore lower back and muscles in my legs, my body was ready for a good upper body workout. That's what I got. I know the routine by heart now so went through the exercises one after another. I usually take breaks between each exercise, but not today. I went through everything. Like yesterday I pushed to the point of being numb and tired but feeling that same feeling of success. So much so that Gretchen and I decided the 3 pounds weren't as challenging as it used to be so we would increase the weight to 5 and 8 pounds. I'm looking forward to the challenge. It's fun to have this feeling again. Wanting to push it again.

1-2-2022

Well, we made it through another year. A year that proved to be the most challenging and difficult so far. Praying for an easy and healthy 2022. Will be nice if The Miracle 3 can see our family have some well-deserved fun and happiness. This would mean the world to me to see this.

I was explaining to Dorene in the kitchen that my wrist on my right hand still burns even after so long.

While in the hospitals my wrist constantly had a burning sensation on the underside of my wrist. I always chalked it up to possibly my arterial line maybe nicking a nerve.

Along with this being the wrist they always put my ID bands on it was always being rubbed and irritated throughout my time away. This kept me from investigating it very closely. Along with the neuropathy I just learned to live with it.

Dorene explained to me that I had ripped the line out and it had laid my hand open. She said blood was everywhere.

I knew about me tearing it out. Many had told me about this ever since they kept me restrained but I didn't know I had torn my hand open. I guess it not only made a big mess but was further cause to keep me restrained. Again, this is something I don't remember. Though I was restrained for about 2 1/2 weeks after I woke up

I began searching for the scar; there had to be one, and there it was. Running about 2 inches from my arterial line scars to the base of my thumb. So, yet another scar I didn't know I had and likely the time I did the nerve damage.

I wonder how many more surprises will be in store for me. Ha! Ha!

1-3-2022

It's difficult to accept that you don't have control of your body. Waking up to a rapid heartbeat, low O2 level, high blood sugar and body pain. Taking so many medications you wonder just what is helping and working and what is being covered up by other medications. I have asked to reduce some of my medications and the response is either they would be stepping on the other doctors' toes or that the medications are a necessity for my health.

Most of these were issued 6 months ago and were supposed to be for a limited time. At least that was what I was told.

I still believe I am over medicated. Hopefully on the 24th with my appointment with my new cardiologist I can at least get the worst ones removed. I hate being dependent upon prescription medicine.

1-9-2022

We are having the kids over for some home-made gumbo. We began talking about our progress on this book and the stories that were in it. The topic came up about how Erin and I both had delusions that were about the cold. I told everyone about being rolled in the Cold Box and looking for my wedding ring and it not being on my finger and how sad it made me. Dorene said, "did you add that to the book because I don't remember reading that"? Erin said the same thing. I told them it still made me sad. Checking back to my notes I saw that it had in fact been there.

Dorene explained that we took my ring off before we went to the ER. I said that I had 2 because one became too small, so we got a second, larger one and did she have both of them. She said yes. This made me very happy. Funny how I'm still learning stuff even today.

Another one cleared up for me was I remembered asking Dorene to take me to the ER the afternoon of June 19th, while standing in the driveway. I was informed it was about 10:30 that night and I was in the bedroom.

1-18-2022

Time to catch up on the last week's events. If that's what you would call them.

I finally made it in to see the cardiologist. This had taken since I got home to get in to see him. Original appointment was for January 24th. I was called by them to reschedule for the middle of March because he had a seminar to attend. My reaction was, he has a 2-day seminar, and it pushes me out a month and a half? I explained I was on 2 medications (Amiodarone and Amlodipine) that my other doctors wanted me off but only the cardiologist can remove them. She threatened to hang up on me because she thought I was too upset. She didn't experience me "too" upset. That would have been cause for concern. I told her go ahead and hang up and said bye. Waiting for her to hang up she came back and said she had a cancellation on February 17th and if that was ok. I said I didn't really have much of a choice so took it.

I was called 2 days later (January 10th) for an opening on the 11th at 2:00. I jumped on it.

After running an EKG Dr. M came in and commented before he sat down that he was aware of my journey and was happy to see that I had survived and recovering well. It was refreshing to not have to go over the history once again and must bring a doctor up to speed on everything. He had read my file and was up to speed before meeting me. Was feeling better about the relationship I would have with him.

Dr. M. then removed the 2 medicines from my list that I had been trying to get off since October. Another reason to like him.

He had seen the history of heart issues from the time I was in the hospital and under sedation but nothing in the recovery stage that warranted the medications. My EKG was normal so he put me on the smallest dose he could of Metoprolol and called it good.

We had discussion on my general health and how I was managing everyday life.

Before leaving he turned his chair directly looking at me and told me God had a purpose for me and maybe it's to put my experience and journey in a book. He thought there would be a lot of interest in it all.

A theme that has carried through many of my doctors. I am surprised how many don't take credit for my survival but give the credit to God. And to stress the importance of finding my purpose from all of this. Hopefully this book is part of it.

We have lost more family and friends over the past week. It just never ends.

This continues to make my mind drift into the world of my own mortality and what effect it would have should I not wake up one morning. I know this disease has taken a significant tole on my body. It isn't healing as well as I had hoped it would at this point. I wonder what is going on in my body to make it feel as though it is only half working.

What will Dorene do? Granted at this point I do very little to help. She is remarkable in her energy to keep up with everything. It's time for her to slow down. We are working towards her retiring shortly so we can spend time together just in case.

02-02-2022

I haven't written in a while. The regular news of people we know continuing to pass away from Covid is taking its toll on our family. The discovery of new variants more infectious than the ones before splits the population on everything from vaccinations, to gathering, to mask wearing. Covid in our area is worse now than it's ever been. Gives me great concern to go out into the public. We are very careful how we go about our daily routines. As long as there are people out there not concerned about their fellow man I don't expect to see much of a change.

Today we lost my brother Tom. Having battled valiantly for a month he finally gave himself over to the Lord. Our family has a reputation of being stubborn and sometimes maybe a little invincible. We tend to react to situations with the mindset that nothing is going to dictate to us what is going to happen. We decide what we are going to do. I reacted this way in ICU for some time until my mind cleared, and I realized how dire the situation with me was.

I find several parallels with Tom's experience. He however was able to check himself out of the hospital against everyone's advice only to return a day later realizing he had made a mistake. This may or may not have contributed to his inability to recover I don't know. But I don't think it helped at all.

Returning to ICU he managed to improve enough to be moved to an intermediate room where his vitals began to improve, and things were looking up. Then complications began to pile up and he was returned to ICU. The following morning, he fell into cardiac arrest and after a time of trying to save him he passed away at 12:56 pm.

Still reeling from the news, I find this difficult to write about yet therapeutic.

Tom's daughter has had such a difficult road through all of this and with her so far away it's very difficult not being able to be there with her. I'm still not able to travel but short distances and she is about 1200 miles away. Not having been there throughout his journey I can't speak on his care or state of mind and not wanting to invade his daughter's privacy I won't go into the details of his stay. I was hoping to get a chance to get to talk to him about his experience. I thought sure I would get that chance after he showed improvement yesterday.

Tom lost his wife about 10 years ago. He naturally has spent this time depressed. Not sure he ever really recovered from this. I'm not sure how anybody could. Some solace the family gains is the belief that he was ready to see her again and let himself go to be with her.

I know from my experience and if I was given a choice to exit the cold box and give up or fight, I would fight. Not seeing anything on the other side of the doorway but a hole in the ground and a cheap pine casket I found no reason to go through that door. But if I were Tom and saw my wife on the other side of that door I certainly would pass through. As a believer I can see how he could stop fighting so quickly. He was in a similar state as me while being sedated. I don't know that it was the same drugs being used but I do believe the experience could be similar.

I tend to gauge these experiences with my own. Draw parallels from theirs to mine. When doing this I tend to conclude that eventually with the many similarities they will ultimately survive and share their story with me. This however hasn't been the case. One of my conclusions is that we give in to the vision of loved ones and are ready to be reunited with them.

There was an acquaintance of Dorene's who just passed away at the age of 63 just by saying he was ready to go. Again, not knowing the whole story I'm not sure how this was allowed. He had his wife by his side. How can a person so young make such a decision and be considered to have a clear mind? Maybe they just have a different make up than me, but I would (and did) fight for every minute I get to spend with my wife and family.

So, is it just physical makeup that saves us or loses us? Is it the difference between facilities and the level of care we receive or as simple as God giving us the option to decide? I believe in Tom's case as well as my own we were given the choice. Not knowing enough about the others, I couldn't say.

I will say the level of care Erin and I received was probably the best we could have expected. Even with my families' differences with doctors and administration we all agreed that the people who cared for me were extraordinary.

I got to spend over 4 hours on the phone with my brother Tom just days before he got sick and another half hour early on in his stay in the hospital. Conversations I am so thankful for and will never forget.

2-22-22

I waited until today to write since my test results would be in from my primary doctor and my pulmonologist.

January 28th was a covid test for the upcoming respiratory function test. Only allowed to take this test if you passed and had to be in isolation until you were. I also took this time to have a required Xray of my lungs since these were both done at the hospital. I also had bloodwork drawn on February 5th for my primary doctor.

This may sound a bit boring put it is an important part of the journey. These results have a direct effect on one's psyche. Already reeling from my brother Tom passing away suddenly I really was hoping for some good news. It appeared to be leading up to some. Seeing my primary on the 7th of February he seemed relatively pleased on my progress. My A1C was a little high at 7.8 and my weight up a little bit but with the problems with my left leg and the cold weather he understood.

I then went for my Pulmonary function tests. This was the one I was most excited about. This would confirm the progress I thought I had made and help me in determining what my future possibly had in store.

A very nice lady pushed my wheelchair into the testing room and explained what the tests were going to be like. I explained that I was nervous about the tests and that it had been a tough road to this point. She said she knew about me and said I was famous in that hospital. I was surprised to hear this since I had only been in their ICU for about 3 days.

She had me sit in a booth and do several series of blowing air and taking air in. Some long breaths and some blowing air out as fast and long as I could. She complimented me on what I was able to do and said she was surprised at how well I did. Another reason to feel a little better but not the actual results. This would come from the pulmonologist today.

Dorene and I arrived on time to the appointment and waited for my name to be called. I sat there with controlled excitement. In the past these were times doctors would say I had exceeded their expectations, and everyone left happy, and I would feel rejuvenated knowing my work was paying off. Today however wouldn't be one of those days.

We began with the nurse walking me in the hallway wearing a pulsox to establish how quickly my O2 level would drop and what my sustainable level would be. I didn't feel I did as well here as I did the last time, I wasn't showing improvement with my stamina but managed to keep my O2 at an acceptable level the short time I walked. Around 85.

I returned to the room where my doctor was, and he began showing me x-rays from ICU compared to the ones I just had taken. Pointing out the absence of the pneumonia. It was a huge difference. So far, I was feeling pretty good. Then we began talking about the pulmonary function tests. Doctor pointed out in the x-rays how there was an extreme amount of scarring that took place in my lungs. This scarring was causing my lungs to only have a capacity of about 30% where it should be at least 80% at my age. I'm sure previous bouts with pneumonia and legionella also contributed to the scarring. He said I was likely to be on oxygen the rest of my life. This was like a punch in the gut. I couldn't find any words to respond. I think he saw the disappointment in me and followed up with exercise and lose weight. This will help you improve from where you are. He would see me again in 6 months and have a better idea where we might be in the future.

We discussed briefly how ECMO is being used less and restricted to people under 50 years old. And if I had been in the second wave, I wouldn't have been given near the treatment I did. This makes me wonder what kind of treatments Tom received. Doctor again stated God kept me here for a reason. If I had gotten sick at any other time I wouldn't have survived.

I have read many articles lately from nurses to doctors explaining how they feel the need and do talk the families into letting their family member go. It just doesn't sound like they are interested in the long haul anymore. I don't understand not exhausting everything to save the patient. One such article was from IU Health Ball, Blackford and Jay is with Elyse Scott and 11 others, on or about 9-15-2021.

I found many parallels in my stay with the issues they discuss in their article. I understand at least from what I have read and experienced I may be some sort of unicorn only because I had the benefit of having not only extended care in the ICU but record-breaking time in the ICU. Was this fair to other people needing the machines I was using? I think any family that thought their family member had a chance of survival would want to take that chance.

They gave my family the same speech they gave families from the article they wrote and convinced these families it was best to let them go. I think the difference was my family didn't accept this alternative and would accept whatever the outcome was, just give me the chance.

The article is a good read and the nurses here deal with these situations on a routine basis and I am sure they see their share of horrible outcomes. I feel for them. Not a job for anyone but a superhuman. I just worry that after seeing so much death they don't become complacent. Give us the chance to beat it. Even when things may look their worst give us the chance to come back. Give families the information but don't try to convince them to let their family go. Let that be their decision. They should have the option to let them fight. I was given that option and am still alive today.

Again, since I haven't run across anyone like me, I am having trouble understanding how anyone would know what the potential problems would be if they haven't experienced it. Maybe they have but I haven't been able find articles that back up their claims. I can only speak from my own experience and that is to give us a chance.

I know I have taken it easy the last couple of months after such a long battle and it looks like it's time to prove another doctor wrong. I appreciate his candor. It's what I needed to get going again. I initially wanted to feel sorry for myself but after thinking about it I should have been trying to get myself in better shape anyways.

I started today riding my recumbent bike and watching what I eat. Granted it's only one day so far and we won't know the full results for months. I'm looking forward to the challenge. Only good can come from this.

3-13-2022

Approaching the middle of March, I am beginning to see the difficulties ahead of me. With the same difficulties I entered the new year with and a couple new ones.

I have developed what feels like neuropathy around the left side of my chest. Much like a sunburn I suffered in 2014 that burnt me badly. It took many weeks to heal and left lingering pain after healing. This went on for nearly 6 months. This is the only thing I can liken it to. It presented itself the beginning of March.

The more I read about Long Covid the more it sounds like there are many side effects that present themselves months after leaving the hospital. The central nervous system they say is affected and can cause these same types of pain. I will be meeting with the neurologist Monday, hopefully getting answers then.

The second problem that popped up is prior dental work has started failing. 1 tooth and a partial have broken off and fillings are falling out. Part of Long Covid? Maybe. This will be corrected on the 28th.

While discussing this with the dentist I asked about bridges to repair the holes that are left and keep my teeth from moving. His response was "Why"? then asked how old I was. And did I think I really needed that. I told them I wanted to investigate it once the teeth were pulled.

It's like 63 is too old to be interested in keeping your teeth and keeping the ability to chew properly. I didn't understand why he thought I shouldn't be concerned with the bridges.

I continue to have lapses in memory and find myself drifting off into la la land or just having my train of thought stop. My focus totally shifting on to something different only to be brought back to reality after Dorene getting my attention or something startling me. This also another result of Long Covid?

This Long Covid is a new diagnosis that like much of the Covid information is sure to change as more is investigated. I can only go off the information shared currently.

3-19-2022

I have now met with my neurologist and have to say it was a waste of time. Disappointed with the results of the meeting. Nothing was gained.

The reason for getting the meeting scheduled was mainly to address some dental work I have coming up on the side I have had trigeminal nerve pain. I have recently been having trouble with pain and was hoping she had an idea on something to get me through the process. Then hoping she might be able to help me with the continued neuropathy in my hands, feet, and ribs.

Our conversation started off with her commenting it looked like I had a rough time with Covid. Yes, I said. About 4 ½ to 5 months. I said yes. She asked if I had been vaccinated and I responded yes, about 5 weeks prior. Then in a slightly superior voice said, "the vaccine came out in January". A little taken a back Dorene promptly responded that she and Haley had been sick with covid over February and March. This also kept me in quarantine since I was the one caring for them. Dorene had also spent time in the hospital during this time. I'm not sure what the value was it added to the conversation at all. It sounded somewhat personal for some reason. Needless to say, the conversation didn't get off to a very good start. We told her once the waiting periods were over, we did our homework and decided to go with the J&J Vaccine. I see she said. I wish I had been on the ball better and I would have made it clear that the J&J also hadn't proven to be as effective as they advertised it to be and asked her if we should have known this before they did. Doubt I will have this chance as I don't plan on seeing her again.

We then switched to the topic of my hands. I explained the neuropathy and the inability to close my hands. She did what every other doctor does and had me squeeze her fingers. Her fingers were so small I couldn't close my hand around them. She then poked them with a toothpick asking if it was dull or sharp. Her suggestion was to squeeze a rubber ball. I said I have been doing that and every other exercise that's been suggested since the end of August. She leaned towards Dorene and said I should squeeze a rubber ball. By now I'm getting angry. She looks back my way and says I shouldn't be giving up like this. That was it, I had had enough. I told her if I had given up, I would have been dead last summer. I didn't get here by giving up. She had no response to this.

What it boils down to is her solutions were to squeeze a rubber ball and increase my gabapentin. I told her other doctors told me I was on the max allowance of 2800 milligrams. She responded that I could go as high as 5000. This also contradicts what she had said a year ago.

She then said she was prescribing another medicine that she was sending to my primary doctor to prescribe. I found this odd she wouldn't do it herself. I later found out from my primary that the medicine she wanted him to prescribe would have a negative effect on my heart medication and cause my heart to potentially race. A problem I had in ICU. I waited 3 days before I contacted my primary's office to see what he might know. The response was he refused to fill the script and said filling it would be up to her discretion. She ended up just increasing the dosage slightly of amitriptyline. So, she didn't make any improvements there either. When it comes right down to it, she was worthless to my situation.

It would be nice to locate people with the same issues as me and see what direction they went to get good help. I haven't met anyone yet in my particular situation. I Have spoken to many who have had covid and even had lengthy hospital stays and even though many of our backgrounds are similar I haven't met anyone who has been through everything I have. Finding a doctor that had managed to help them would be nice also. Here they seem gun-shy to go outside their comfort zones. I am not feeling Freeport will have a lot of the answers I seek.

Haley did however bring up a good point (as she does) I have been ahead of schedule ever since I woke up. Who's to say it isn't just my body making a correction and putting me closer to where I would be normally. I do agree I pushed myself beyond my comfort zone to get home. Much harder than I do now. I do these days find it harder to keep that pace. Weather it's my ambition or just what my body is capable of these days, I don't really know. I should be on a regiment. I want so much to get back to normal. The coming months will tell the story. I'm expecting more improvement as I go. I certainly won't quit. Here's to hoping I get a chance to add a second, more upbeat, sequel to this book.

3-20-2022

I was sitting up very early this morning revisiting conversations I had with the nurses and staff at UW preparing for an interview with their Patient Experience Consultant. I remembered a conversation with a nurse but not from ICU. It was from the first week at Select. I don't remember her name and I only ever saw her this one particular night and only for a short time.

We discussed how I was feeling, and she knew of my story and did a good job at lifting my spirits as she went through her steps checking my vitals etc.

I explained the frustrations being bed ridden and how I appreciated the PT and OT getting me out of bed and trying to teach me to walk again. She said, yes, you know though it can always be worse. There is a young man she cares for who's only 19 and has had a bad motorcycle accident running from the police. I believe she said it was simply trying to get out of a speeding ticket. I could see in her face she was deeply disturbed by this. I was stuck trying to find something to say. She continued with a conversation she had with the boy.

The boy was paralyzed from the neck down. He was asking her if she thought this was permanent. Would he ever walk again? She told me she didn't know how to react to this. She knew he wouldn't. It was clear this was likely how he would be the rest of his life. I remarked that God would have the final say and she smiled. I said he pulled me from death. Miracles do happen. She said she told him it would take a lot of work and not to give up because it will be hard. I said, what more can you say? She smiled, patted me on the shoulder and disappeared to the hallway.

I'm not sure if this was more beneficial to me or her. I think equally both of us. I understood after our conversation how my situation could be much worse.

I find it increasingly suspicious I never seen her again. Nobody mentioned her. I did see on the news The following evening the story of the boy who had the accident. But was she real? Was she an angel there helping me through a difficult time or even a vivid dream? I figured if I saw it on the news there had to be some reality to it all.

I do believe it's the doctor's responsibility to deliver this type of news not the nurses. I think the nurse did exactly what she should have. Nobody should completely dash a person's hope regardless of their situation. **dum spiro spero, (while I breathe, I hope).**

3-23-2022

BITTER BUT

I could be bitter about the time I have lost

But I've become more grateful for the time I have

I could be bitter about the pain I live with

But I'm grateful getting closer to God who gives me strength each day

I could be bitter about my physical challenges

But I am grateful for slowing down and enjoying life

I could be bitter not being the guy who fixes everything when it breaks

But I am grateful to see my children step up and become the strong, independent adults they have.

I could be bitter I'm not the husband I was before I became sick

But I am grateful for the new, more powerful relationship I have with my wife.

4-5-2022

It appears my coughing fits have returned. Not constant like in the past but fairly frequently. It feels very much like it did when I got home. The changing temperatures Spring has brought I expect to be a contributing factor. It's been cold and damp. I have tried to spend time outside which may prove to be a mistake. I hope at least it isn't anything more than that. I still don't have the power I used to have to cough normally. We have also just received our second booster shot though other than a sore injection site there haven't been any issues.

We worked on Dorene and Haley's chapter last night and I was introduced to many more events over Summer I had no recollection of.

More who had passed on and more about my mental state and behavior over my ICU stay. I'm surprised they didn't try to send me somewhere else. This will be covered in their notes. I am disappointed in myself for my behavior. I didn't think it sounded like me.

I hadn't planned on writing much more figuring the changes would be slight and uninteresting. But I thought the return of the coughing could be significant not knowing what the future holds. After all this is how this all started.

May 10, 2022

Dorene and I made a trip to Madison to visit Haley and decided on the way home to visit the hospital I had spent so much time in.

The ICU room was difficult to find. My memories of room 5 were mixed with reality and delusion. My view out the window was in great contrast to the view from outside. It appeared to me from inside the room looking out to be an entrance to the hospital. I used to watch the people coming and going and thinking I was seeing family members on their way to visit me. Only to be turned away because nobody was allowed entry to the Covid floors. These clearly were delusions. I even saw my late Uncle Wayne heading out of the hospital. Looking from the outside in It became clear this wasn't an entrance to the hospital, but a parking garage and they were people walking towards stairwells to head down to sidewalks to take them to the entrance. It still gave me comfort at the time thinking family and friends were making attempts to come see me.

Below the garage floor and directly out my window they were putting in what appeared to be a reflection garden of some sort. It was coming along nicely. They planted a hydrangea tree the end of August or first of September. I liked this as it is one of my favorites and have planted them at home. The men planting it dug a hole, dropped it in, gave it a little water and left. I thought cool, I can watch it grow.

Time went by and I noticed it wasn't receiving any care. No water. It began to whither. Weeks went by and the tree looked all but dead. I even found out that the tree represented an employee named Kelly who has passed away. This really bothered me. I complained to everyone who came into my room about it needing water and attention. They tried convincing administrators to give it some attention. They said it was getting enough but I knew different. I watched that tree every day and this was not the case. Others considered sneaking out there, but the area was pretty secure.

I would pray for rain and would sometimes get a little but not enough to save it I didn't think. I hoped it would go dormant early with the cool weather coming hopefully saving it.

Room 5

Next was Select. I had a room on 2 different floors. The fourth floor second from the left and the third floor third in from the right.

I was moved in the middle of the night without warning. Had me scared for a bit not really knowing where I was being taken. Turns out the third floor is less restrictive and apparently I was in better shape than expected so I was moved to a less restricted floor.

I could see into my old room from my new one. Gave me some entertainment looking into the window and seeing what the new patient was watching. I also had a better view of the parking lot so I could watch on the days that Dorene or the kids would come to visit.

June 9, 2022

It has been a year now since our family began our journey through Covid. A journey I have grown so tired of. Reliving those nightmares while researching for this book have made me weary. I wanted to complete this project before a year was up. I was giving myself that year to heal and come to terms with the new me. Most of my memory for the previous year and a half gone. I occasionally have a memory return and have tried to capture them here. But now it's time to stop.

There was a time I didn't think I would reach this point. To be here typing this is fulfilling. The year is done. Gone forever. It's time to focus on the future. I don't plan on looking back any more than absolutely necessary.

Erin was taken to the ER on the 15th and me and Joshua on the 19th of June 2021. It has changed our lives forever.

Thank you for showing some interest in our family's story. It's been difficult for us to share and revisit. We have so much ahead of us and an entirely different approach to living it. Our son Ethan and his fiancé' Aurora will be getting married July 9th. Something else Covid caused us to postpone. Dorene retired and we are planning our new lives together. The future looks pretty nice.

My overall health has improved greatly since getting home and doctors reports have been good for the most part. Though it has slowed me down and made use adjust our plans for retirement Dorene and I are still planning on traveling and having family gatherings. We refuse to let Covid stop us.

Life is still challenging in a lot of ways but between all of us life has drawn us all closer (if that's possible) and given us direction on just what is important. My scars are a grim reminder of my battle but also give me a sense of peace knowing they represent the best things in my life also.

Life is God's gift. Now on to tomorrow.

June 19, 2022

It has been exactly one year to the day that Dorene had taken me to the ER at FHN. I promised myself back in the ICU that if I was ever lucky enough to reach this day, I would no longer look back at 2021. I believe at this point though not fully rehabbed I have still defeated the disease that tried to kill me.

My health is good for everything I have been through. My doctors are happy with my progress, and I have been adding new exercises and walking further each day. I don't believe I was this health conscious before I became sick. My diet is better also.

My goals for the future are first and foremost to recover as much of my lung capacity as I can. We already know that it won't be all of it but every little bit helps. My O2 recovers quickly so they are working the way they are supposed to but with only 30% capacity they run out fairly quickly. I walk 1 to 1 ½ miles twice a day now. This takes multiple standing brakes along the way and at this point in my rehab is a good workout. I add steps at the beginning of each week. Hopefully reaching the 5K this coming year.

Tomorrow I'm to visit UW TLC South and get to personally thank those who saved me. Something that means the world to me. This will make my future officially begin. The last thing on my to do list from my previous year.

Becky from ECMO arranged this reunion with the nurses from UW Madison TLC that took care of me. She has been such a wonderful friend in keeping in touch. I am really looking forward to sharing and hearing the stories of my stay.

6-20-2022

The big day is here. And it was an amazing reunion. Emotions are high with this one. These beautiful people took the time to visit with Dorene and I. This was also the first time I had been in public and visited a public establishment in over a year. I was nervous until I saw Becky. I knew once again I was in good hands.

Becky, Megan, Kelsey and Janyne showed up. I guess there were a couple of elderly gentlemen near us that were jealous of the fact that so many beautiful women were sitting with just one guy. I got a kick out of that,

We talked in length about my stay and how things had finally slowed down in the ICU and the Covid world. We kept the conversations light.

Sometimes you have these types of reunions, and they never quite reach the level of excitement as you might expect but this was not the case. These women were just as incredible as how I remembered them. They are amazing.

There was talk of having a group of survivors reunion someday. This would be wonderful. A chance to meet more people like me.

Becky, Megan, Me, Kelsey and Janyne.

Becky would later send me a picture of Kelly's Tree. The hydrangea I was so worried about, and it was beautiful. It apparently survived the winter and came back strong. Another miracle from Room 5.

7-31-2022

Today has special significance to our family. This date my Mother passed away at UW of all places in 1993 and our Nephew Mike in 2013 in Alabama.

This has always been a day to open the drawer in my mind and get out all the memories and lovingly sift through them. As much as it hurts the memories are a nice escape from the current challenges I am having.

When I finally was able to come home my challenges felt at times insurmountable. The therapy was hard. Just getting from one room to another was very difficult. I have managed to get past most of that. My Doctors at that time looked at me in amazement. An anomaly of sorts. There was much praise and belief I would continue to progress and be a success story. It was a good feeling to have that support and belief in me. I wanted to impress them just like the places I had been previously. It kept me motivated.

Fast forward to today and I have improved. I had been walking a mile in the morning and 1.2 miles in the evening. There were standing breaks along the way and knees and feet hurt but I pushed through it. These distances I worked up to over time, but things were looking up.

My last doctor's appointment with my GP didn't go well. My weight was basically unchanged and my blood sugar and A1C was too high. I decided one thing I could do and get better at was walking. Good exercise too. That and a better diet should put things back in order.

As I began walking and watching what I ate everything gradually started to fall into place. I was feeling good about myself and was motivated again.

Then on July 20 I began to have Afib issues. This went on for 4 days straight. I had seen my Cardiologist on the 19th and had no issues then. This is a reappearance from way back in ICU. I hadn't had an issue since. Why now? Because of the walking?

This has now sidelined me from my one good exercise regiment and slowed me down.

My meds were increased on the 20th, and on the 29th I visited a heart rhythm specialist. This visit was another disappointment as he told me the only way to fix this problem was with an ablation. OK, I said. I have had 2 of them before, lets fix this. He said no, with my diminished lung capacity I would never come off the ventilator. It was not an option. I asked about if my lung capacity should increase where would it have to be to be enough. He sighed and said we would cross that bridge when we get to it. He clearly wasn't confident I would ever get there.

It definitely seems like the newness of my survival and recovery has worn off and reality is settling in. Doctors are franker with me now and are very straight forward. I guess since I proved I would survive they now want to push me. I like that but in turn I think they want me to accept things as they are. Not to expect much improvement from here on out.

He told me I would have these Afib issues the rest of my life and medications are the only option I have. In the future if it continues to be a problem then I may even have to return to the ones like amiodarone that come with a higher risk. Not something I wanted to hear. He was being straight with me. It's hard to listen to the bad news but not the first time I have had to deal with disappointment.

It appears, at least so far, the meds are working. I plan on returning to my walking regiment tomorrow morning 8-1-2022. I'm looking forward to it. I hope my body is up for it.

Each of my doctors on these last visits were critical of my health. Each had a concern that maybe I wasn't doing everything I should be to get to the best I could be. I suppose their right. The "kit gloves" have been removed. Time to suck it up and get moving.

My next appointment is in August with Dr. Q the pulmonologist. This is a big one. Have my lungs improved? I have worked them hard. I have gone places and on walks forgetting to turn my concentrator on and managed very well. I sit outside and in my chair without supplement oxygen and still manage to keep O2 above 91. I am hoping the continued walking will help me with my overall lung health. It will never be normal but pushing to have to use as little O2 as possible.

8-2-2022

Picking back up on the walking is proving to be difficult. The layoff combined with the August heat is challenging. Humidity plays a part also, but I seem to handle that better than the other stuff. My lungs are still the biggest problem.

I have walked twice already today equaling about 2 miles. Hope to get another walk in tonight once it cools off. The second walk proved easier than the first for some reason. This is 2 days now in a row without Afib issues and I am able to exercise. Can hopefully continue and even add some things to the regiment.

8-5-2022

I was hoping by now I would be done with updates and just working towards the best version of me I can get to, but steps forward seem to be bringing equal steps backwards. I believe the new medications are causing fatigue. They are to keep my heart from going into Afib which they have but in turn I haven't had any energy or drive. It stormed all night and into this morning so getting out wasn't an option but yesterday I couldn't get myself going. I was tired and hurt all over. Doctor Kz thought it would be a short-term effect and once I adjusted, I would be back to where I was.

It seems that if I miss a couple days my body reverts back weeks and I must build it up all over again. I need to be better than this come appointment time with the pulmonologist.

We have set up an appointment in Madison August 9th with a professional message therapist. Haley and Dorene seem to think it's worth a try though I'm not sold on the idea. I expect the results will be about what mine are. I spend the day stretching my hands and feet to where I get them to somewhat improve by evening and by morning they are right back to where they were.

8-9-2022

Now the beginning of new chapters. Dorene and I have started making plans for traveling. Starting out slow of course. We are very excited with this new chapter of our lives. It's incredible we have made it this far. We will have been married 40 years come November 20th and 1 year September 7th with our vows renewal.

Dorene and Haley took me to the massage therapist. It was a relaxing experience, though not sure much was accomplished. I could have gone much longer than the 45 minutes because it was so relaxing.

When she finished, I could feel the hamstring in my left leg taut amongst all the relaxed muscles. It was an odd feeling, and I could tell it at least played a part in the pain in my left leg. I don't see any improvement in my hands, but I didn't expect any there. I went there for my knee and neck. And what she did, it helped in those areas though not enough for the expense of a two-hour drive and the cost of the massage itself. We will still check other avenues.

Received a picture of the hydrangea tree that was outside the window of Room 5 in TLC from Becky. It was remarkably in full bloom! So, it had survived the winter even after its poor treatment even up to that point. This made me very happy to see.

8-17-2022

Got to meet my new Neurologist today. What a difference. We will call him Dr. M.

We found him to be very knowledgeable. And well versed on the issues I came to him with. He began with naming my condition as "Critical

Illness Neuropathy". I had never had anyone put a name to it before. He had even given dissertations on the subject.

Doctor described how and why it effected the nervous system especially in the extremities., neck and brain. This is onset in the first 2 weeks of illness and since I had been critical for such a long time, he expected my recovery to take much longer and be much harder. Finally, some reality to my situation.

He was impressed on how far I had come. He was also impressed that my cognitive thought was good and that I didn't seem to have any lasting brain damage or fog.

He told us of a formula used to calculate the time of recovery. Taking several measurements such as age, height, weight, and the time you were critical along with other factors. Again, since I was critical for so long my recovery time would be more like 30-36 months. Most likely the 36. This was far more time than the original year I had been quoted in the past, however it gave me a better sense of where I am 9 months into it. It sounded much more realistic. Another point for the new guy.

The healing starts out rapidly starting at the spine and gradually working out to the extremities. The further it works out the slower the process is. This would explain why my hands and feet have shown far less improvement. This was why I made the decision to leave my former doctor and seek someone more in tune with my situation. I am not falling behind on my recovery; I am right where I should be or even a bit ahead. Feeling some better now.

He couldn't guarantee a full recovery but would expect much more improvement for the future. Some nerves will require a lot of time to repair themselves and in some cases reroute around dead ones and regrow. This is a long process. Nerves grow very slowly.

We then discussed the high levels of medication my previous neurologist had me on and how I refused to increase them. He agreed that if they didn't work on the high level I was at that increasing them even more wouldn't help.

After review we concluded I would try something different and return to the original dose of the gabapentin originally prescribed for my trigeminal neuralgia.

I am regaining a little faith again after seeing him and even though my lungs probably aren't going to get much better my quality of life has a chance.

8-19-2022

Left knee pain has become unbearable so went in to see Dr. B.

Did an Xray and found the bones of my knee to be in really good shape. No signs of needing a knee replacement in my future. This means it is soft tissue or cartilage damage. He believes it could be a meniscus tear. This is something I did to my right knee years ago and the pain is very similar.

Since I have a stimulator in my back, I can't have an MRI for further diagnosis. He has fitted me with a knee brace and set me up to see an orthopedic surgeon on 9-2-2022.

My A-Fib has gotten progressively worse and I made contact with Dr. M. and he doubled my dose of Metoprolol. We have arranged another appointment with Dr. Kz to follow-up on the med increase

8-22-2022

Polo Revisited

We pulled into Polo from the north on Route 52/26. This turns into Division Street. Continuing south towards downtown and turning left onto Mason Street. Familiar places such as the grocery store on Division and Mason Family Restaurant on the left.

I never paid much attention to the downtown so there wasn't really any recollection of the buildings or storefronts. Our business there was just Masons once in a great while or the chiropractor a block off downtown.

Mason Street is a one-way street with diagonal parking. Old pictures show it was diagonal parking way back in the horse and buggy days. The parking was generally full when we went there not giving us much view of the storefronts.

We went to the chiropractor and she did some amazing things. She adjusted my neck to the point I could turn my head to the right which I had been unable to do. Then worked on my wrists. That gently moved things back into place. I have never had that done before. I am always appreciative of anything that will help my hands. It did nothing for the neuropathy but did do wonders for my wrists.

When we left the chiropractor we decided to go back around the block and look closer at the downtown. We parked right where my delusion of the burned-out building was. It was an eerie feeling sitting there. It was all coming back to me. Seeing my car sitting in the smoldering rubble with bricks piled on it.

Dorene pointed out to me an empty lot at the end of the block. She said there had been a fire there where I pictured my car about 15 years ago. She said 2 large buildings there had burned down. I didn't remember ever hearing about this but that's no surprise. I thought it strange the 2 buildings I saw that burned down actually did. Was it something hidden in an old memory? If so why would that particular one be the one to visit my subconscious? This gave me an uneasy feeling.

This is the actual article about the Polo fire.

It then dawned on me, I stumbled to a bench across the street. I asked Dorene to look back and see if it was there. She replied "yes". This gave me a chill. I finally got my seatbelt undone and managed to turn and look back. There it was. Just as I had seen it.

We sat there for some time, mostly quiet.

One building was a café I hear and the other had been used for storing junk as far as I could find out. My car stored in with a bunch of junk. I guess nobody would look there.

The lots were turned into a nice sitting park I suppose for tired shoppers. It was a nice small park.

The park where the buildings once stood.

I continue to read about Long Covid. Some doctors believe it, some are believing most everything these days is a result of it and then those who don't believe it at all.

I have read that the majority of the studies are results of studying charts or reading reports. Not actually interviewing the patients. Dorene thinks this is where the studies need to begin but now in its 3rd year, I would think this is something that should have already happened.

We have been keeping a closer eye on my Long Covid symptoms and think we have a handle on what I have at least experienced.

First would be my memory. We already knew my memory of 2021 and much of 2020 is nonexistent. Though bits and pieces have been coming back to me. We notice short term memory has been a problem. Dorene reminds me of conversations we have that I have no recollection of. She's sure I have problems with this.

Next is pain. My hands and feet especially hurt. This Dr. Mo contributes to Critical Illness Neuropathy and is still a result of COVID.

The swelling in my feet comes and goes. It's the same in my hands. To walk all over again is very difficult. Still not stable even before I hurt my knee.

Next, I'm finding my body doesn't accept physical activity like it used to. I have tried since April to gain strength in my arms and legs and continue to have setbacks. Currently it's my left knee keeping me from walking. Hoping to figure this out on 9/2/22.

My teeth have cracked and broken off, and my caps have come loose and broken off. My teeth hurt constantly.

As for general breathing, we know my lungs have capacity issues; but some days seem to be better than others. I expect this won't change much. I at least hope it doesn't get worse.

My stamina has been a huge problem, especially since I've gotten home. Your mind believes you can do things, and your body says no. This also comes in waves.

Until I hurt my knee and began having AFIB issues, I thought I was improving. Since then, I seem to have digressed to the point to where I started. All that work gone.

My eyesight has changed from nearsighted to farsighted. I wondered why my glasses didn't work. I needed a new prescription!

AFIB has become an issue, and this one I don't understand. I was good up to the point I started pushing myself. Once I did this the AFIB kicked in. though medications have been increased, I still have breakthrough episodes.

Another frustrating problem is Brain Fog. I believe this for the most part has cleared up. I still have focus issues. Especially when listening. Conversations are difficult.

Sleeping is difficult, as I suffer from bouts of insomnia, though not as bad as in the Spring and early Summer. I also dream a lot, where before I rarely had dreams.

Another issue is Depression, although I'm not sure if that's what I would call it. I get tired of the same routine I'm faced with every day.

My hair has finally gotten the oil out of it and is now soft.

Dizziness happens some days when getting up or laying down. Not so much lately, but in early summer it was quite frequent. Doctors say it can last a few weeks to a few months. Mine has been 9 months and going strong; however, they do remind me that I am not an ordinary case.

I went for my pulmonary function test this morning. I was not impressed with my effort. It has fallen off considerably since my AFIB restarted, and the injury to my knee has kept me from my walking and cardio.

The good news was Pam (the technician) said my tests had improved from the last time. She wasn't allowed to give me any more information beyond that, as I will have to wait to hear it from Dr. Q.

She says improved but I expect it is a slight improvement. I think she knew I was down about all of it and wanted to give me something to cheer me up a little, and it did. But if Dr.Q. gives me a thumbs up, well, that would mean a lot.

8-28-2022

From the moment I got up today it has been a challenge. My left knee has continued to get worse. It's a good thing the people at select took the time to teach me how to properly use a walker. I should have worked harder at getting proficient at it though. It is currently my mode of transportation.

I promised myself back then that I would never use one, but I currently have no choice. My left knee will not allow any weight on it. Absolutely no support. The pain has exceeded my threshold. A rare occurrence. I believe this pain is contributing to my Afib issues also. Doctors don't really want to prescribe any kind of opiates for pain due to the addictions that come with them, but I have been through the worst of that in my medical history and have been able to work my way through it. So, I understand them being cautious but I am in constant pain. It's becoming overwhelming.

9-2-2022

Dr. B. referred me to Dr. Bl. An Orthopedic Surgeon.

He was a nice guy. Young but knowledgeable. He was very surprised after seeing my scars and hearing my story that I was there. The stories he had heard of people on ECMO always ended poorly. He thought I looked very good for everything I had been through.

Once we went through all the options that we couldn't do we landed on arthroscopic exploratory surgery with a spinal since I can't be sedated with general anesthesia. Since I only have about 30% pulmonary lung function, the fear is that if I am put on a breathing machine for surgery, I will not be able to be weaned off, if I am even able to survive the procedure. He was hoping that maybe everything could be cleaned up enough to fix the problem, and if not may have to have more done in the future.

He gave me a cortisone shot in the meantime and said to set an appointment for a two-week follow-up to see what good it did. It currently is more painful than it was, but he said it could take 24-48 hours for it to kick in. So, I will see him September 16.

I am hoping it is just inflammation and nothing is torn. Not after all of that.

I have controlled my A-Fib. I had been drinking caffeinated sparkling water, two or three a day. I have discontinued all caffeine and my heart has been good ever since. I sure miss the caffeine but not the A-Fib issues that come along with it.

I am hoping in a couple days I will at least be able to walk again. It's very challenging even with a walker or cane, very limited on what I can do.

I was surprised that he thought my knee's bone structure was in incredibly good shape. I figured with how much abuse my legs took over the years, it would be falling apart. All this time it must have been soft tissue/ cartilage damage. I know my right knee isn't the same story.

9-5-2022

It's Labor Day and everyone is at the farm for dinner. The pain in my knee has eased up enough where I can at least walk again. I did have a 4-hour battle with AFib for some reason. And exiting the house at the farm I began having what felt like Charlie Horses in my left thigh. I wasn't sure right away what was going on. I was just hoping I wasn't having a stroke. It was an unusual type of pain. I was feeling pretty bad by this point, exhausted, light-headed, and still trying to manage my way to the car with a barely operational left leg.

I got too the car and Dorene took me home. Once in the door, I had some water, took my pills, and went and laid down for a little while. I should note that when we left this morning, I grabbed the wrong daily pill pack so when I went to take them at the farm, the container was empty. So, I was late with the morning dose of heart medications to control my heart rate and try to keep me out of A-Fib.

My heart rate was high at 153 and I was sweating profusely. I crawled into bed and had a fan turned on me and it felt good, and I was able to relax.

I wasn't able to find anything I had that I thought would have set off AFib other than I had overeaten at the family gathering and was late on my meds.

At about 7 pm, I got up and went to sit out on the deck. After a few minutes I took an ECG and I was back in sinus rhythm.

9-7-2022

Well, we made it! 1 year since we renewed our wedding vows. A year of ups and downs. Even though my challenges lately have been many we still managed to get out and go to dinner.

For our first 20 years of marriage, we went to Lino's for dinner. Our favorite place. The best atmosphere and easily the best pasta you could ask for.

It had been almost 20 years since we had been there so on Dorene's birthday we decided to go. It was the same magical place we remembered. So, we decided to go on our 1-year anniversary today.

I was still feeling weak, but the experience was great. The same great atmosphere and same great food. We will hopefully return. Maybe for our 40th in November.

My entries here have become mundane and repetitive. Just describing maintenance of me that I expect will continue on and show little if anything new and interesting. This might be the right place to stop.

It has been 1 year since I woke up. A year I have tried to document. I hope you found it interesting and am happy you decided to take an interest in our stories. We are glad we managed to create a record of our experiences and writing this book was a very beneficial experience for us. We are also happy that credit has been given to those amazing people who kept us around to be able to produce this.

So, this is goodbye for now. Thank you for showing interest in our story. These Angels mentioned here are the reason we were able to write these stories. Our gratitude just isn't enough to praise the work they do. They are the true Superheroes. And speaking of praise, God deserves the ultimate glory for putting us with so many amazing people.

With God ALL things are possible. I'm living proof of that. We have faced evil. Paralyzing fear. You could say the Devil himself and survived. We will now experience and enjoy life one beautiful day at a time.

JOSH

Initially, Josh was a bit hesitant in sharing parts of his story, as we all process trauma differently. It is hard to talk about, sometimes. But he knew the importance of his story to this project and wanted to be a part of it. This is his story, as told by him, and recorded by Erin.

This experience was kind of like a nightmare I couldn't wake up from. The nights were the hardest, because they felt long, and never-ending. I would think up scenarios of how I could escape, or get myself released, and then would be sad when I realized there was no way I could leave.

I went though a very dark period of time, where depression set in – deep – and it lasted for months, even after being released home. I found myself turning off my phone because I couldn't bring myself to speak to anyone or even respond to messages. It was too overwhelming, and I had too much going on in my mind.

I was worried about myself – would I survive this? I wasn't improving, and there were few answers as to why. Fortunately, God put me in the care of Kate Kinney, NP. She realized there was something wrong, and immediately sent me for a CT Scan. It was discovered that there were PE's (Pulmonary Embolisms) in my lungs. She placed me on Warfarin right away, along with the Lovenox/Heparin Shots I was already receiving daily. My wife Erin always says, "God Bless Kate Kinney!" She truly was a Godsend.

I was worried about my wife. I had been told that she was in all likelihood not going to survive this. She had been declining quickly and had been placed in a paralytic coma and intubated. The hospital in Monroe, WI realized they were unable to do anything more for her and had her airlifted out by helicopter to St. Mary's in Madison, WI, in hopes that as a bigger hospital they'd be better equipped to handle her critical care.

I was worried about my Father-In-Law. Would he be okay? He was so sick. How were my In-Laws handling his illness? Were they doing okay? It was a constant roller-coaster with his health, and it was definitely an incredibly stressful time for all, waiting and praying for answers.

This period of my life really showed me how we take things for granted; simple things, like feeding yourself and being able to use the bathroom and clean yourself on your own. You suddenly needed help to do everything you once could, because you were too weak to do it yourself. You have no privacy and no choice in the matter, because you know you need help. Fortunately, the medical staff was amazing, and kept your dignity as much as humanly possible.

Because of this, the song "Way Maker" means so much to me. There's a verse that goes, "**... Even when I don't see it, You're working, Even when I can't feel it, You're working, You never stop, You never stop**

working." Even though I couldn't always see God working, or feel His presence, I knew He was there working in our lives. I had to have faith that He was there with us during this dark, scary time, and that things were going to be okay for us all. God soon showed how Great He is, as I am now fully recovered, and my wife and Father-In-Law are here, still with us. Three miracles.

I also wanted to note that even if I couldn't talk because I was on constant breathing assistance (either via bipap or vapotherm), I still enjoyed having visitors. It helped with the hopelessness and loneliness I was feeling, and it was my connection to the world outside, which was still going on despite my world being completely derailed.

One thing that was a highlight to me was that I really wanted to see the fireworks on the 4th of July. My CNA Katy wheeled me down the hallway and out the door and watched them with me. It was so nice to be outside my room, and be able to have some normalcy for the first time in weeks. Katy knew how important this was to me, and I'm so thankful she volunteered to take me.

Two days later I was released to go home. I would need supplemental oxygen and was going to be staying with my parents while I recovered so that I could have the extra help I needed. While I was waiting for the discharge papers, I started to get nervous. It was taking a while – had they changed their mind? I asked my parents who were there to pick me up, "Am I still getting to leave today? Did they change their mind?" My parents reassured me that I was still getting to go home, and not to worry. It just takes a while to receive the discharge paperwork. A little while later, we were on our way!

Now it was time to adjust to life outside the hospital with the limitations I was still dealing with. Bathing, eating, walking with oxygen all required assistance or measures I hadn't had to take before. Not only this, I still wasn't able to travel much other than to the doctor. I do want to say I am so thankful for my parents for allowing me to stay with them for my recovery, because it allowed me to get out of the hospital when I did, and I could not have done any of this without their help.

Fortunately, my wife was awake now and was improving daily. She no longer needed intubation and I was able to speak with her when they brought a phone to her in her ICU room. This helped, because I knew she was still here and was improving. After another couple of weeks, she was transferred from Madison back to Monroe, which was only about 25-30 minutes away from our home, allowing me to actually visit her. It was a surprise to her, and she cried when she saw me – for the first time in a month. It was an emotional, great day, and it was so good to finally see her in person.

DORENE AND HALEY TIMELINE

Although some of the following may, at times, seem critical and anger-driven, please bear in mind that this was written to reflect the highly emotional state of mind felt during what was the most stressful period of my life, to date. And I am expressing thoughts that may not be rational now, nor would they have been rational prior to these events. There are some, however, that I stand by. I want to be clear that this is intended to be informational and factual. It is not a work of fiction. It is from personal perspectives.

In the end, please be assured that we are grateful, beyond measure, (and I apologize for not getting all facility and staff identification perfectly named) to the staff at FHN, who recognized Kevin's urgent need for transport and securing care at UW Madison; the TLC South TEAM at UW Madison, including Nurses, ECMO, Physicians, PA, Pharmacy, RT, PT, Environmental Services, and many others; Select Specialty Hospital Staff- all; Van Matre Rehabilitation- all; St. Mary's Hospital PICU staff and others, and SSM Health Network Monroe Clinics and Hospital staff and their Chaplains.

We would like to recognize the County Health Department for their tireless efforts and concern during this and the following periods that we worked with them. Their staff was not just doing a job. They truly cared about the outcome of those they served in their community. When they continued to contact us during the convalescence of ourselves and loved ones to assure all of our needs were being met, in any capacity that they were able to assist, that tells you that they are special people!

And how could we forget our pharmacy staff who did more than their part to assure meds were able to be dispensed at home to family members, when I was out of state, by setting up my ability to pay remotely. They also allowed other parties to pick up medicines, with my phone approval, since there were frequent quarantine issues and when out of state with family members in hospitals, we often were not available during pharmacy hours. And I know many prayers were said and staff followed the family medical page on social media. I know there are so many who played key roles who are not mentioned and I apologize, it is an unintentional omission.

Sometimes in life we talk about good versus evil. In this scenario, it's clear that evil presented itself in the form of a virus- at minimum. We also talk about guardian angels. Whether or not you believe in a physical manifestation of such entities, I believe there are clearly forces that are beyond our understanding. Certainly, the Bible and other sacred texts declare it is fact. And, certainly, those forces were at work in our lives throughout these experiences.

And I want to thank my daughter Haley, who helped keep me sane throughout this journey. Many people have graciously listened to my story and credited me with being strong. I credit Haley with keeping me on track, or I might not have been able to make that journey. Her role is greatly underestimated.

Above all, we are grateful every day, for this God-given "second chance" to celebrate life as a family!

Sincerely,
Dorene

DORENE

We'd been cautious. I always social distanced and wore a mask as prescribed. We seldom went out to stores, had groceries delivered, did drive thru for prescriptions, and rarely ventured inside retail establishments. I worked in a very small office group and, again, we wore masks and socially distanced whenever we did go into the office- otherwise, working remotely. But, presumably due to the fact that I took some immunosuppressants and corticosteroids for inflammatory issues in my body, I contracted a thick mucosal pneumonia in the lower lobe of my right lung. I wouldn't have known it was pneumonia as I didn't have normal respiratory symptoms. A CT to diagnose the abdominal pain caught it. Although I had a 104 temp, I tested negative for COVID-19, but was, none-the-less placed on the COVID Unit at the hospital for 4 days. Once the fever was finally brought under control I was allowed to go home. It was then that I began to exhibit signs of fatigue and heavy coughing. And 2 weeks after my first symptoms, Haley tested positive for COVID. She was VERY sick. Kevin took her to the ER. She was given chilled IV fluids and monitored for 6 hours before being sent home. Her illness and fever persisted excessively. Throughout our illnesses, Kevin took care of us and never got sick. He even got stuck being quarantined through the end of February due to his re-exposure.

As time marched on and Haley's recovery finally was reasonably complete, family "debate "occurred as to whether or not to take the COVID vaccines. Even health care seemed divided as to efficacy of mask wear and vaccines. To be honest, I still have reservations concerning mask wear as it pertains to most masks that are worn and their efficacy. As far as vaccines, information continues to change with such rapidity that it boggles the mind. Initially, we understood perhaps because that is what we were led to believe, that vaccinations were starting most effective phase at 1-2 months post vaccination. We selected Johnson & Johnson not just because it was a single dose but because it was less like the mRNA than the others based on the charts we referenced. We did not like what we feared the implications of the mRNA vaccines were.

Our middle child felt she wanted to take the Moderna vaccine because she did want the mRNA protection.

Our oldest child was not eligible to receive a vaccine because she was on high dose steroids and a biologic. Due to her ineligibility her spouse opted not to receive a vaccination.

Our youngest child chose not to take a vaccine at that time. His fiancée did get vaccinated, and while she had some of the potential strong side-effects to the vaccine, her father actually had an allergic reaction to the vaccine. This caused him to end up in the ER with anaphylaxis and he now carries an epipen.

Now April 2021 has rolled around. Haley decided to go to Indianapolis over Memorial Weekend to meet friends and wanted to be vaccinated so she can fly, so starts the Moderna series, which she completes before travel.

We lost our nephew, Scott, in February 2021, to what we believe was an unexpected, massive heart attack. A family gathering for his memorial service was also planned for Memorial Weekend in Alabama, so we made arrangements to attend. I can't say whether it was due to travel plans, or the ravages we had seen of the Delta variant on TV, but Kevin said to me one evening that he felt he needed to get the vaccine. He said he didn't think he would do well if he got this virus.

I admit I was inwardly surprised. For all our discussions I really didn't think that he had wanted to receive the vaccine, but I was not going to deter him from receiving a vaccine he felt would help him! So, I simply said- Whatever you feel you need to do we will do.

We, as a couple, had debated the little-known side effects of the mRNA vaccines. We had never been anti-vaxxors. But something about this entire covid virus and its vaccine- both releases- angered us. It was political and manipulative on a scale that we had not witnessed in our adult lifetimes. It wasn't that we doubted that the virus was real. And the masking policy, such as it began certainly wasn't sufficient to prevent the spread of much of anything except animosity among free thinking individuals who understood science, psychology, and socialism. Too strong? All those thoughts were certainly tossed about, discussed, and if mentioned even casually in the wrong company, got you beheaded on Facebook, or worse.

Suddenly it was taboo to ask in my place of business whether or not you were vaccinated. That swiftly changed to you WILL be vaccinated, or you WILL be terminated. You WILL COMPLY.

But I digress…

Kevin and I received the J & J vaccine on May 15, 2021. We had few to no side effects. I had a sore arm. We got our vaccination cards and away we went. We were cautioned that it wouldn't be fully effective for about 2 weeks. So, we should continue social distancing and masking protocol.

We went to Menards the following week and Kevin wasn't going to wear his mask. I reminded him that he was only one week post vaccination. He groused about "why did we bother to get vaccinated if we still have to wear these stupid masks"? I threw up my hands and told him he was an adult and could make his own decisions. But he put one on while grousing all the way to the door.

On June 3, Kevin and I got away for a weekend together, something we hadn't done since 2017. We went to Dickeyville Grotto in Wisconsin and then to a little cabin on the Mississippi River in McGregor IA. You could watch the barges, fish, listen to the train, plus the cabin was adorable. The cabin sat literally between the railroad tracks and the river. The trains were active and loud. We knew the tracks were there when we booked but underestimated its round the clock activity and whistle blowing. But we grew accustomed to it- mostly. We even squashed coins on the tracks! We shopped in the little town, had Mexican for lunch in a great little bar/restaurant, went to an antique shop where we both felt a really weird, heavy sensation upon leaving the lower level of the building and almost hadn't the energy to get up the stairs. It was very strange. We didn't actually mention it to each other until later.

A terrific novelty/bookstore there had a wonderfully impertinent line of greeting cards. This was right up my alley- suiting my sense of humor. I selected one for each member of our family based on their personalities as there had been one speaking to me for each.

The following day we went to Guttenberg Iowa to the Farmers Market. Lots of close contact. No masks and no practice of social distancing outside. It's a lovely town.

It was a hot day. Stopped in Galena in the evening for supper. Went in a little bar downtown. Great food and not crowded.

The following Wednesday and Thursday were our son Ethan (June 9), daughter Samantha (June 9), and our Daughter Haley's (June 10) birthdays.

On June 10th, our kids (minus Sam) gathered at our house to celebrate the birthdays. We had a fun evening and with much hilarity which is common when we are able to get three kids together. Kevin wasn't feeling his best and as is often the case retires to his recliner in the living room, rather than sitting with us at the dining room table. He says he isn't comfortable in the dining room chairs due to his back and hip pain, for which he has a pain stimulator implant.

The next few days saw our rock garden finished and the roof to the SHE SHED porch got done. Kevin was pushing himself so hard over the last couple weeks to do several projects and kept indicating he needed to complete certain things – projects – like he was on a mission. I kept saying it isn't like it must be done today!

On Saturday June 12th, we were invited to Ethan and Aurora's house for their first cook out at their new house. It was a nice day and Ethan was stoked to have us there. Haley was absent, as she already had plans. I decided to call Mom (Joanne), Dad (Gary), and Chad to see if they wanted to come, as they had not seen Ethan's house yet. They had just gotten over COVID, contracted in early May. Fortunately, they had mild cases – probably not the Delta strain. However, it did cause Mom to get pancreatitis and Dad who has post-polio syndrome struggled through his pneumonia while trying to remain active so as not to increase his chances of blood clots. My Mom was advised by her doctors NOT to receive the vaccine due to severe allergies and intolerances to most all medicines.

Since it was already after 1pm they had already eaten, and Mom wasn't feeling well, so I told them we would see them another time. That turned out to be a good decision.

Hamburgers and hot dogs were cooked and served. Josh left to go to a family reunion. Erin stayed because of her intolerance to the summer heat, and the fact that she wasn't feeling well. She said she felt her allergies were flaring up.

Later that evening, after returning home, Erin alerted us she had gone to Urgent Care and the staff said she was to be treated for bronchitis and upper respiratory infection, and that they had swabbed her for COVID as a precaution. That was Saturday night.

On Sunday night, Ethan went to work, then went home early as he was feeling awful, which is very uncharacteristic.

Around 1am on Monday morning, Erin's MyChart posted a positive result for COVID-19. She notified Haley, who notified us.

By that afternoon, we acquired and distributed home testing COVID-19 Tests to all seven family members. Four of the 7 of us tested positive. Erin, Josh, Ethan, and Kevin were now all positive for COVID-19. Dorene, Haley and Aurora tested negative.

CHAIN OF EVENTS NOTES GATHERED FROM TEXT MESSAGES, EMAILS, FAMILY MEDICAL UPDATES, FACEBOOK AND WEBEX CALLS

1-15-2021

Dorene not feeling well. Went to the doctor. Started antibiotics. Not tested for covid as a kidney or bladder issue was actually suspected. No apparent symptoms for covid.

1-16-2021 Through 1-19-2021

Haley took Dorene to ER at FHN. Fever 104.2. Admitted but tested negative for covid. CT scan showed heavy pneumonia in lower lobe of right lung. Still placed on the covid floor. BP was 91/42. IV started with antibiotic Levaquin. Veins swollen, red and arm began itching. Still couldn't keep her fever down. Allergy noted. New IV antibiotic required. Respiratory therapy was required to try to break up the pneumonia, but coughing was difficult to produce, no urge.

The illness was never diagnosed as covid, but in late March an antigen test proved I had covid sometime earlier. After four days in the hospital, my fever had subsided sufficiently for release.

FHN Hospital staff was incredibly kind and proficient in their duties and care-giving.

My illness had evolved and presented quite differently by the time I had been released hospital. I had a low grade fever, then the deep, barking cough developed, the tremendous fatigue and brain fog that did not abate for several months.

I had a previous history of pneumonias, but had both pneumonia vaccines in 2017 and 2018, per Mayo Clinic, which we understood were supposed to protect for 10 years. So, if COVID, it took that long to evolve into an illness that seemed recognizable with the cough, or I came home from the hospital with it, having been exposed there- though in retrospect, I do not believe that to be the case. But I believe Haley became infected from her exposure to me. I was off work through 2-1, then worked from home for another month due to quarantine of family members.

2-1-2021

Haley had a low grade fever of 99.7° that night and started to have fever shakes.

2-5-2021

Tested positive for covid and received the call from the county health department case worker. Called into work and explained the diagnosis as well as went over contact tracing within the workplace.

2-9-2021

Kevin took Haley to ER at FHN with a high fever and difficulty breathing. Fever did not respond to home treatments and she was unable to breathe if she moved out of a certain position while lying in bed. Spent 5 hours in ER and given breathing pills, along with cold temp IV to reduce fever. She was given Tylenol, Zofran to stop the dry heaving, heart meds, bloodwork, an electrocardiogram, and a portable x-ray. Bloodwork showed evidence of the cytokine storm as her C-Reactive Proteins and D-Dimer levels were extremely elevated. If D-Dimer had been just a few points higher, she would have been treated for blood clots.

The x-ray technician told her it didn't look good but said he couldn't actually tell her the diagnosis. (After checking her file, she found that the reason for being unable to breathe was due to both lungs showing signs of localized lung collapse.) Her O2 was 82 but she was not put on oxygen. Then for some reason she was sent back home. Had she not been "young and strong" they might have tried to keep her. She was prescribed a standard antibiotic, 2 breathing treatment pills, one steroid pill, 2 inhalers (albuterol and fluticasone propionate), and supplements.

She fortunately recovered and returned to work in early March.

When having a follow-up appointment with a Nurse Practitioner at the respiratory clinic, the NP was dissatisfied with how Haley's ordeal had been handled at the ER and happy to know that she was improving. Hospital space was certainly at a premium during that period. And, we thank God that by His direction, the difficult decisions her health care team was faced with making, along with our home care, and her good sense, her lungs were able to recover, although it has taken over a year and she is not yet able to achieve pre-COVID functions. This is a critical issue for Haley as she is a vocal performer and holds a degree in professional vocal performance (although she holds a full-time job in another field and performs vocally, for pleasure through various avenues).

Kevin cared for both Dorene and Haley without getting sick. He was also quarantined longer than both of them getting released February 26th.

5-15-2021

Dorene and Kevin get the J&J vaccination.

6-10-2021

Family Dinner for kids' birthdays. Kevin felt tired and had to lay down after washing Haley's car.

6-12-2021

Cookout at Ethan and Aurora's. Erin had a slight fever and not feeling well, but attributed it to seasonal allergies and asthma. Josh was not feeling well either, but also suffers seasonal allergies and is asthmatic. Since he had family visiting from out-of-state, he opted to leave and visit with them.

6-13-2021

Erin to ER in Monroe. Swabbed for covid. Ethan left work sick (3rd shift factory). Erin returned home from ER.

6-14-2021

Erin's test returned positive around 1 am on the Patient Portal system, a computer system for communication between health network and patient.

All six remaining family members took home rapid covid tests. Josh, Ethan, and Kevin tested positive. Dorene, Haley and Aurora were negative.

Dad took Ethan to ER at FHN. Kevin took Ethan because he had also tested positive for covid. Kevin waited in the car for Ethan because you weren't allowed in with the patient. Ethan was sent home with the standard collection of meds. He mostly had body aches, fever and stomach ailments, although he did lose his sense of taste and smell. He also had tremendous fatigue. He was so very fortunate to recover quickly. He completed his quarantine and was able to return to work, still "angry" that as a young healthy man he couldn't bear the illness burden for his other family members.

Dorene came home from work and worked from home due to quarantine policy. Haley was still permitted to attend her place of employment based on the county regulations and her health status and temperature on a daily basis.

Erin admitted to hospital after second ER trip, due to difficulty being able to take deep breaths. Haley, having dealt with this in February counseled her to go to ER immediately. Her O2 saturation was very low and she required supplemental oxygen and additional medicines.

6-15-2021

We had been corresponding with Erin through text messaging and she suddenly stopped responding to messages. Unbeknownst to us, Erin had been moved to ICU and put on bypap as her oxygen saturation levels were getting worse and worse. We assumed she was getting some needed rest and let it go at that for the night.

6-16-2021

We had no communication from Erin this morning and were finally able to track down her whereabouts in ICU, where I told the nurse that I was relieved she was getting the help she needed and was able to avoid being intubated. He hesitated and told me that he was sorry to say that she was headed that way as soon as he could make all the appropriate arrangements. He then asked if she had a living will and medical POA. I told him she was married, and I did not know about the arrangements since the wedding, so I pulled the family together and within 30 minutes we had a family Zoom meeting with Erin, Josh, the doctors, Kevin, Ethan and Aurora and I- right at our dining room table. Erin specified that she wanted all life saving measures utilized and that her husband, Josh, was to be the primary medical POA, with me as his backup. When all was recorded, we shared our love for each other, verbally, and allowed Josh a moment with Erin. What an awful feeling to speak with a loved one by phone, knowing it may be the last time- not being able to physically have access to them due to COVID protocol!

While we assumed that intubation means she will stabilize and heal, that turns out to be the furthest thing from reality. We go on with our day, tenuously, awaiting word on progress, abiding by the adage 'no news is good news'- right? That there's nothing to tell. Well, not always. There were major complications during the intubation process due to her physical structure. The process took an extensive amount of time during which her oxygen saturation levels dipped dangerously low, 40-50%, for extended periods of time even after getting her on the ventilator. When the decision to fly her to St. Mary's was made, they were fearful she would not survive the flight.

Haley and I are at the chiropractor when I receive a call from a tearful Josh, brokenly telling me they were flying Erin to St. Mary's in Madison because the intubation process had not gone well, that her O2 'sats' were in the 40-50% range and they did not think that she would survive the flight. I told Josh we were on our way and that we loved him. We rushed home to discuss a plan with Kevin and Josh. When we got home Josh had already gone to their home to be alone and try to process the information that he may lose his wife. Already being sick and feeling less strong than he would otherwise, Kevin was also grief-stricken with the news that he could lose his oldest child. This was probably the hardest I have ever seen him take news of any sort, which I attribute, in part, to his weakness from being sick.

At that point, like most parents I believe you start playing the bargaining chip with God. 'Well, Lord, if you could just take me instead of Erin- please! She is young and has so much living to do yet!' But if that were the plan you would have been in that bed to begin with, right? Well, maybe not.

It was decided it would be a good idea if Haley and I could be near Erin in Madison until things stabilized, so we packed up for a multiple day stay, then left for Madison. Upon check-in at the hotel, I spoke with Dr. Hernandez who made it perfectly clear in a kind, but firm manner that Erin was extraordinarily sick, and that it was very uncertain as to whether she could survive. And, if she did survive her prognosis for recovery after having suffered oxygen deprivation to that extreme was a great unknown. This will cause you to have tremors erupt in your water glass and have you convinced you have early onset Parkinson's or a rare Midwestern earthquake has just taken place. These are not the tidbits you hope to hear upon trying to retire for the evening.

A mother's love is endless...

6-17-2021

I enter St. Mary's PICU ward unwittingly around 10 am, hoping that rounds would have been done by then and I could get some information. I had hoped to meet with Erin's doctors and determine her current health status and treatment plan. Since I had presented myself to the PICU unit, which occurred because Erin had not been labeled as a COVID patient yet in the records, I was able to see Erin through the glass of her ICU ward. It was a relief to see her, even though she is facing away and in prone position. A nurse was working with her, and she was connected to SO MANY tubes and hoses. The charge nurse gave me a brief rundown and led me to a waiting area where she assured me that after the doctors had made their rounds, one of them would be out to talk to me. However, it could be an hour or so. Through a series of miscommunications and delays of many hours, I went back to the charge nurse, and she informed me that I would not be allowed to enter the PICU unit anymore as I wasn't able to be in Erin's room and I wasn't allowed to stay in the hallway. And the new COVID rules prohibited me from being in the waiting room. Therefore, once I met with the doctor staff, I would need to leave the building. All communications would be done by phone from that point forward. Until she had passed the 28-day mark from her original positive COVID test she was quarantined from us.

Her care at this point was to keep her in prone position as much as possible as that created least pressure on the lungs. Give her broad spectrum antibiotics, and all other CDC approved drugs for COVID protocol. I was told she was so very, very sick, not to think beyond the current day.

6-18-2021

Haley and I had checked out of our hotel and were waiting to hear from Erin's doctors at St. Mary's before heading home. We drove to the Arboretum and parked to await the phone call. After waiting for 3 ½ hours, at around 9:30, the doctors finally called after making their rounds. They informed us that Erin was finally in a relatively stable condition to where they thought they would be able to begin working with her.

After the call, we began to feel uneasy about driving the hour and a half home; something was tugging at us to stay in town.

After some deliberation, we decided to try to head home, but after traveling out the way we came into the arboretum, we were stopped by flashing lights on the road ahead. It turns out that with no wind, no storm, and no natural reason, a tree had fallen, blocking the road. With no moon, it was an eerie event.

A Ranger had explained to us that he was waiting for an Arborist to come and remove the tree, they were opening another road for them to exit. This road happened to take us to Erin St., which led us right in front of Erin's room at St. Mary's. We decided this was a sign that we should stay in town that night and did, although no further contact was received from the hospital that there were any further set backs. We stayed in the same hotel, same room we had been staying over the previous several nights. During the night, Haley woke to see an image of Erin floating above her. It turns out Samantha was also visited by Erin's image that night.

6-19-2021

Haley and I received a call from Ethan. Kevin was very sick and Ethan thought we needed to come home to check on him. Ethan found him sitting in his recliner chair but leaning forward crying and really sick, although Kevin, himself had no recollection of the event. Apparently, that was the only position he could get relief from continual coughing. We got back from Madison early afternoon and finally convinced Kevin around 10pm to go to ER at FHN. I waited for him to text me the results of his exam. He told me "the doctor said it was a good thing I came in. I have double pneumonia and will be staying a few days". I texted him that I'd bring him the necessities in the morning. And, I love you. He responded I love you too.

6-20-2021

I received an early morning call from ICU, with staff telling me Kevin needed to be intubated. I asked if I could leave and come up right away to see him and he told me that there was not enough time, that they needed to move immediately as Kevin was really struggling on the bipap and he just couldn't catch a breath due to the constant cough. I knew this situation was BAD, having just experienced it less than a week prior with Erin, and here we were again! I asked if I could please talk to Kevin and was allowed to tell him I loved him. He tried his best to tell me he loved me too, but the coughing was so persistent, and the machines were obviously very loud. I could tell he was gasping and fighting for every breath.

I was permitted to see Kevin in ICU once he had been intubated, the ventilator adjustments had all been made, medications had been ordered and he was cleaned up.

Apparently, Kevin's intubation process had not gone as planned either. He was trying to sit up and felt everything during intubation. This was due to his prescription fentanyl pain patch use history. The fact that my husband has an extremely high pain tolerance and also requires a huge quantity of pain medication in order to be effective was not something they were aware of. This is something I made sure that all medical staff was made keenly aware of moving forward!! I am worried about whether because of how Erin's case has gone whether I should consider moving Kevin to a bigger hospital.

Each day I now get an update on Erin from St. Mary's as Josh gets too flustered because it's Erin, his wife! And he isn't familiar with the medical terminology, and he isn't always able to relate it back to us and answer all the questions we end up asking of him. Therefore, he gave permission for me to get and share the updates with him. I then get the update on Kevin and share both with him. I ask how he is and ask if he has been checked out. I think he is not getting better, and he is very worried to hear about Kevin, in addition to being worried for the Love of his Life!

6-21-2021

I have checked in at St. Mary's and the news is not good. Erin has fluid in and around her lungs. They will continue with all same protocol to try to improve breathing function and reduce fluid.

I have sat with Kevin all morning, except when asked to leave the room for the staff to complete their work. X-rays and CTs were completed to determine whether he may have any blood clots. They told me I could return to his room when imaging was complete, then told me that the Chief Hospitalist wanted to speak with me. I knew that couldn't be good news. I planned with Haley who was at work, so she could be available to sit in by phone when the doctor came in for the conference.

The doctor made no bones about the fact that based on Kevin's condition and what was typical for COVID, that it was expected that he would likely get worse, and they wanted to get him moved to UW Madison as soon there was a bed available at the facility. They felt he was a good candidate for a procedure called ECMO (Extracorporeal Membrane Oxygenation), if it came to that, and he could receive that treatment there. I was relieved because I had a growing concern all day and wasn't sure how to approach the fact that I, too, thought he needed to be moved to a bigger hospital.

I took time to call Josh at one point in the afternoon to update him and ask if he had gone back to get reexamined. He said no. I asked why not, and he said because he was afraid he would be admitted. I told him he absolutely had to get back to the doctor because of Kevin's condition and that he was being airlifted yet that night. I asked Josh to talk to Kevin to say goodbye, because I didn't know if he would get another chance- even though Kevin couldn't respond and likely would not hear, nor remember.

Haley worked late to finish training in case she wouldn't be in the next day, and the hospital allowed her to come in late and sit with Kevin until a bed freed up at UW. I stayed until Haley got there and let her stay until visiting hours were over. Kevin was flown by MedFlight to UW Madison TLC South later that night.

It was pretty late until Kevin got in and they got him settled. I received a contact number for the unit, which I of course called. They said that they would be in contact in the morning.

6-22-2021

At 1:45 am. I receive a text from Josh telling me that he is in ICU in Monroe. I text back, "How did you get there?" He said, " I drove". I was distressed that he drove himself. But it was done, and I did get out of him that his parents were also aware. Then I got no further response from him. That also had me worried…

Kevin's first day at UW. He started at 100% vent. I talked to two doctors about the admission. The goal would be set and reevaluated as often as needed to keep Kevin moving forward. They would get Kevin situated and proned 16 hours. Reduced O2 (oxygen) to 85% to prevent additional therapies.

I was asked if I would like to have Kevin participate in a clinical trial and declined, as I wanted to know what drugs he was getting, and this was a blind trial using Plavix or a placebo in the prevention in the formation of blood clots in Covid patients.

6-23-2021

Kevin 75% O2. Today Dorene is told about the 3 stages of covid.

1. Infection
2. Inflammatory
3. Fibrosis vs Recovery

Or ECMO, or transplant, or both.

5-day antiviral and antibiotics end today. Steroids will be continued 4 more days. Stable to slight improvement overall. On back, temporarily reducing paralytic to allow muscles ability to oxygenate. Infectious control will be looking into strain.

Erin O2 stats now in the 90s. Ventilator has gone from 90-80-70-60%. Still fever over 103 with an unknown source. Broad spectrum antibiotics.

Josh able to eat a small amount today. Tried the vapotherm machine but O2 drops significantly since he's a mouth breather so went back to bipap use. Still running a fever and are giving him steroids.

6-24-2021

Removed paralytic and reduced the sedatives from Kevin. O2 vent now at 60%.

Erin at 12:30 am. Spoke with nurse. 103 + fever which is lower than yesterday. Treating with Tylenol and cooling blankets. No big changes.

Monroe Hospital Chaplain- A wonderfully special someone worth mentioning. May God bless her.

Facebook Update:

Per the late-night call with both Madison hospitals: Erin's fever was getting too high (over 103) and they were using cooling towels and medication to bring it back down. As she had just finished her initial treatment of antibiotics, the fever going up, has her team doing many tests to determine the cause, as well as putting her back on a broad spectrum antibiotic.

Dad's sedation was lightened so they could ask him some questions and he could answer by nodding his head. They were able to lower his oxygen levels on the vent a little. The doctors reminded Mom that he is by no means out of the woods but was showing slight improvement. The infectious disease team is looking into what strain Dad has because of how many family members are all having the same issues, he is fully vaccinated, and has been around Mom and I when we both had COVID-19 with no issues prior to vaccination back in January/ February 2021.

End Facebook post.

As time went on, I (Dorene) read an article about the fact that due to legalities and also regardless of whether a patient has the variant or standard covid-19 virus, the treatment protocol is the same. So, there is no reason for a patient, nor their doctor to know the strain. It is only necessary for public health officials to know so that if there is a concern or public health emergency they can advise. Therefore, we never learned what strain Kevin, Erin or Josh had.

I also read an article concerning scientists being able to determine whether a person would survive covid-19. The article went on to outline comorbidities that stated a medical facility, in a triage situation, could use this information to move on to the next eligible candidate for treatment. Additionally, it noted how this was also helpful for the insurance companies.

Yes, the insurance companies want to dictate who is eligible to receive treatment and how much they will pay for it. How much is a life worth? Ask your health insurance company. I bet they will have an opinion.

6-25-2021

Kevin-New fever and increased oxygen needs. New antibiotics and proning.

Josh in better spirits today and able to talk to family by phone through his mask.

6-26-2021

Erin-Dr offers cautious optimism. Off paralytic and positioned on back for last 48 hours. Maintaining good oxygen stats and wiggled toes on command.

The staff is now asking more questions about her health beyond the immediate critical situation. Although they obviously have her health records, we talk about her diagnosis of Hidradenitis Suppurativa (HS), one of the health diagnoses that was a reason to be taking the biologic medication, which was the reason she did not pursue COVID vaccination for herself. HS is a painful dermatological condition which causes boils, abscesses, sinus tracts, often leaves open weeping wounds and subsequent scarring, and is usually located in areas that are prone to sweating, i.e. armpits, groin, etc. It is not caused by unclean skin, is not acne, is not contagious, and is often difficult to diagnose initially. (More information is available at aad.org) We ask the staff to be sure areas they may not be checking, in skin folds, etc., are carefully monitored. They already had wound care team working with her. Of course, they are aware of diabetes, IBS with evidence of Crohn's (but unable to diagnose due to use of low dose steroids), Rheumatoid Arthritis, Osteo Arthritis, GERD, Asthma, High Palate.

Josh still somewhat discouraged. 75% O2 on bipap. Tolerates vapotherm 10-15 minutes.

Kevin-100% vent support required again due to new infection.

A longtime family friend came and brought supper to Haley and I. A real morale booster at a really low point for us.

Mom, Dad Chad, Uncle Ray, Cousin Tim make the drive (85 miles) to move Rusty to Mom and Dad's house. Rusty was recently diagnosed with stage 4 metastasized lymphoma. This will be a multiple trip event over multiple days/weekends.

Facebook Update from Dorene:

Josh is still doing about the same. Nothing new to report. Still seeking prayers.

Erin had a slight blip yesterday where she was breathing quickly and hard. They aren't sure of the cause of that event but they adjusted her vent settings and were able to calm her down. The staff told Mom it is hard for COVID patients on ventilators because the sensation feels like you are suffocating. It is hoped that a patient will be weaned in a short time, and it is important to keep the pressure settings lower than someone who is on a ventilator for permanent use, so as not to damage the delicate tissues while they heal and the pneumonias disperse, in this case. The patient must stay relaxed enough to let the ventilator do the work while the lungs rest and heal. Since breathing is an involuntary function, when the body seeks to try to take in a breath and cannot successfully do so, the mind panics. It is obviously one of your very strongest natural functions and even though the blood has been properly compensated with adequate oxygen by the ventilator machine, not being able to inhale causes you to feel as though you are suffocating. They do have Erin on anxiety meds as well as pain meds to help keep her relaxed. (The very same is true for Kevin.)

Dad (Kevin) had an issue yesterday where they did not understand why he was suddenly having issues with oxygenating. They found the cause was secretions in the upper respiratory tract and they had to increase his sedation to suction everything out. His oxygen intake had started around 50% but had increased to 90 – 100%. After cleaning his airways he was able to go back down to around 65% intake.

Saturday June 26, 2021 Updates:

Erin had a good report today. Her doctor reports that she has been able to be on her back for the last 48 hours and maintain her oxygen level. There has not been a need to use the paralytic medications currently since her blood oxygen levels have improved and that has allowed her to be able to respond to a command to wiggle her toes! We were thrilled to know she was able to respond. She is doing well with eliminating fluids currently and her ventilator settings seem to have been adjusted well to make her comfortable at this time.

Josh is making progress on the vapotherm machine which only covers the nose. It is more difficult than the bipap machine he has been using which covers the nose and mouth. He is down to only 70% oxygen need from the machine now and that is a wonderful improvement. He is still fighting a little fever yet, so aren't sure when he will get out of isolation but will remain in ICU.

Kevin has had some significant setbacks. He has developed a fever and gone back on 100% ventilator support. His X-ray indicated a thick substance in his lower lungs now and secretions filling upper airways. Samples were collected and sent to the lab in hopes of identifying a bacterial culprit so specific antibiotics can be used rather than broad spectrum. Still waiting for COVID strain identification.

6-27-2021

Kevin-5:30 am. Pneumonia has worsened with a lot of secretions. Requires a lot of suctioning. Has a strong cough. O2 sats 91-92. Vent at 100%. Labs and vitals good.

It is not the first, nor will it be the last time, that I wonder if Kevin has made a pact with God to trade himself for Erin in a covid bed.

Mid-day- Bronchoscopy ordered. Although this morning when the Facebook post was written, ECMO was not yet a reality, by midday it was determined that ECMO (VV) was to be placed in Kevin.

The doctor that talked to me about ECMO cautioned me that ECMO would be a potentially difficult roller coaster ride. Gains made one or two days in a row may all be lost the next. Then the patient would make gains and again lose ground, the cycle repeating over and over. Looking back, I would say that was an accurate, yet inadequate statement.

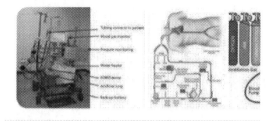

ECMO stands for **extracorporeal membrane oxygenation**. The **ECMO** machine is similar to the heart-lung by-pass machine used in open-heart surgery. It pumps and oxygenates a patient's blood outside the body, allowing the heart and lungs to rest. ... For patients recovering from heart failure, or lung failure or heart surgery.

https://www.ucsfhealth.org › extraco...

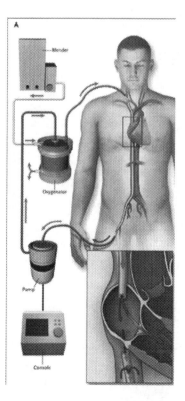

Erin- Opening eyes, Squeezing hand. This is SO ENCOURAGING. And while we are praising God she is still with us, we must take everything one day at a time and not get ahead of ourselves, nor take anything for granted.

Josh- Still low-grade fever and O2 support. Praying he is soon able to kick the fever so he can start improving from the rest of his symptoms!

Facebook Update 6/27/2021 (from this morning):

Kevin's pneumonia has worsened. He is continuing to receive Tylenol for fever, antibiotics for infection, steroids, 100% oxygen on ventilator, other support and of course has heavy sedation. He is able to produce a strong cough which allows for suctioning to remove the heavy secretions. We are told it will be a long process. They are going to perform a Bronchoscopy on Dad to try and clear his lungs and see what is actually going on. From there, we will determine the next course of action. There is a potential he may need to undergo ECMO treatment.

Erin is doing well and even in sedation is able to cooperate, react on command, open her eyes and squeeze her nurses' hand. They turned her oxygen down because she was actually getting too much oxygen so her lungs are doing better.

Josh's oxygen was able to be lowered from 70% down to 55%, and he was able to sit on the edge of the bed for 10-15 minutes. He is finally out of isolation!! He is still in ICU and can have one visitor per day.

6-28-2021

Kevin is stable but very critical following the ECMO installation yesterday. There were issues early today with a slowdown of blood flow through the ECMO machine, and therefore poor blood oxygenation. The Team had to turn the machine components by hand while others hurriedly worked to replace the entire machine. Then they continued to monitor everything to determine if tubing, clots, or some other unknown was the problem or if it was fixed. The problem did not repeat, so all is good for now. An Angel was there again today.

Erin- Small improvements in insulin requirements.

6-29-2021

Kevin- X-Ray shows even worsening pneumonia. Tracheostomy needed soon. PIK line put un upper left arm.

Erin- Still tests positive for Covid. Requires 21 days of isolation. Down to 50% O2 vent support.

Josh- Baby steps but improving. 45% O2 on high flow mask.

Facebook Update:

I want to make it clear that while there are small progresses being made be Erin and Josh they are still in critical condition and in ICU. We take small victories day by day, as my Dad's condition has shown that things can change very quickly. Please remember this when updates are posted. We are still praying for miracles and we are still not anywhere near out of the woods.

Josh's Mom saw Josh in hospital today and he is doing better. Josh was positioned on his stomach, was able to reposition on his back, and staff also sat him up and use regular nasal canula oxygen to eat lunch. His oxygen remains at 98% throughout entire lunch and he was able to feed himself! She prayed over Josh during her visit. This was the first time she heard Josh say he was fighting to get better and that he wants to go home! She is thanking Jesus for this miracle!

6-30-2021

Kevin- Very slight improvement. Trach placement a couple days away. ECMO tweaks continue.

More wakeful and trying to interact.

60% O2 vent. Labs meet goals.

My good friend Linda comes by with pet supplies and road trip snacks and quick meals.

7/1/2021

Dorene goes to Monroe Hospital to visit Josh.

Josh moved to general care room.

Facebook Update:

Apologies for the delay in updates. We have been very busy trying to take care of things at Erin and Josh's house as well as figuring our how to take care of bills without having their credentials.

Mom will be seeing Josh later today and we will have a more recent update after that. As of yesterday they thought he was almost ready to be out of ICU and transitioned into the regular hospital. He still relies on the bipap machine for oxygen overall but was able to eat with a nasal canula without any major decrease in his O2 levels.

Erin seems to be making some more small progresses though she is still testing positive for the virus. They were able to wean her off the nitric oxide and are going to test to see if she can breathe on her own without the ventilator so they can avoid doing a tracheostomy. They seem willing to extend her time on the vent for a short while if she is close to being ready to breathe on her own, even though prolonged throat ventilator use can cause permanent vocal cord and other damage. I believe that was in today's schedule for her.

Dad is still very sick and it seems the pneumonia refuses to back down. His most recent X-ray showed that it was still getting worse. He does intermittently respond to commands to squeeze a hand or wiggle toes but he tired quickly under the sedation and drifts in and out. When we talk to him and the nurses via video chat, he will open his eyes and occasionally blink. The doctors have decided that he will need a tracheostomy sooner rather than later and will likely happen by the end of the week. The ECMO is still doing its job and we continue to pray that by giving his lungs no work they will begin to clear and heal.

Josh's Mom spoke with the nurse 7/1/21 and she verified Josh got moved from ICU to his regular hospital room 104 this afternoon. Please check with Julie before visiting to schedule your date as it is one visitor per day.

Josh is on the vapotherm machine during the day and bipap at night and for sleep. They are trying to keep him awake more during the day so that he will sleep better at night. She is thankful for each victory that Josh has, and while she knows he still has a ways to go, knows God can turn it around quickly!

7/2/2021

Erin remembers waking up.

Dave W, one of Kevin's good friends from high school calls, as Dorene hadn't gotten back to him yet, and he was worried. Bless him- and the many others who have reached out.

Trach installed on Kevin.

Facebook Update:

Big news for Erin- she was able to be taken off the ventilator yesterday (Thursday July 1st) and placed on a bipap machine for breathing! She is doing well and as her sedation levels are lessened has been able to respond by nodding and wiggling fingers and toes!

Kevin is still in respiratory failure. Lungs continue to be bypassed by the ECMO machine which something like one would think of when you think of kidney dialysis, but for the lungs. One large catheter is inserted in the neck vein and another in the groin vein, with a machine intercepting the blood to filter, oxygenate and pump in the middle. He continues to receive oxygen by ventilator- a separate machine- to keep his lungs dry and viable until the nasty virus wears itself out and goes away.

Today he is scheduled to receive a tracheostomy so the ventilator can come out of the throat. It will then be attached to the tracheostomy externally. It should be much more comfortable with less risk of infection. It's going to be a long road, God willing. And there are NO assurances.

We hope you all have a wonderful 4th of July weekend with your loved ones! Please don't take them for granted.

Take good care dear friends.

7/3/2021

1pm – Medical team meeting for Kevin at UW.

From the 1pm Medical TEAM Meeting: Kevin still in respiratory failure. Lungs continue to be bypassed by ECMO. The team feels he can recover from this. However, it may take a significant amount of time for the lungs to clear, perhaps a couple months due to the virus, fluid and inflammation. No way to know for sure so need to be patient.

Erin converted to high flow nasal cannula like Josh. Is at 60% oxygen and is not requiring other types of meds. Restarted nutrition through tube until throat heals. Too early to determine intellectual effects yet. They're allowing her 2-3 days more to fully wake up. We talked about her not knowing about Josh and Dad, and that she should not yet be told. Started physical and occupational therapy today, 3 hours a day. Social worker called about sending orders for eventual discharge to rehabilitation facility. Said to be sure that rehab knows she is unaware of Kevin and Josh, and that they should assess.

End Facebook post.

Dorene's reflections:

After the Medical team meeting they escorted Haley and I to Kevin's Room 12. Although probably a breach in protocol, but because of his extremely critical condition and poor prognosis, both Haley and I were permitted to enter his room together. When I saw him in person for the first time since he left Freeport, I felt weak, felt like sinking to the floor and weeping. But I'm not a drama queen, and that would be too dramatic for me. But, Oh God! He looked so vulnerable, my strong husband. Yes, he has been through a number of surgeries over the years. But this wasn't like any of those times. I could see so much that the view over the i-pad camera had failed to reveal. His skin color was very poor. The home haircut and beard grooming we hadn't gotten around to before he got sick, left him shaggy and unkempt looking, the gray/white now obscuring the remaining darker hair. The hair was pushed straight up and spiked out above the head band that supported the large, clear plastic hose from the ECMO machine, filled was with his blood. That hose was attached by a catheter to a large vein in his neck, then sutured in place. That hose came straight up past his ear toward the top of his head, which curled around and fed from the ECMO machine where filtering and oxygenation had taken place. The cycle was the completed with the opposite end of that hose connecting through a catheter in the big vein in the groin, also sutured in place. There was, what seemed like a mile of hose coiled in between, filled with Kevin's blood, being cycled through the ECMO machine and him, keeping him alive. Although I was touching it through a double gloved hand, I could feel the warmth of his blood in that hose.

His teeth and gums were bloody, there was still a fair amount of blood seeping from the ECMO sites and the newly installed tracheostomy insertion site.

He literally had two banks of IV pole machines, each with at least four pumps. Of course, he had to be restrained to prevent him from dislodging any of these precious, lifesaving lines, even involuntarily.

I look at him lying there and I can't even touch him with my bare hand as he is in quarantine, and I am fully suited up in PPE. I think that this could be the last time I see him, and I can't even touch him! But I do touch him gently where there aren't tubes and wires and monitors- hoping on some level he might know I am there and that it might help him fight. At this point he was not conscious. I left this encounter feeling extremely deflated and numb, as low in the hope department as I had probably ever felt in this life.

7-4-2021

We talked to Erin on the phone, and she talked back. Still very hoarse and voice very soft and her mind cloudy from sedation, but seems to be her sweet, loving, witty self. Was moved from ICU to intermediary care. Complains of being "Hangry" (so hungry it makes her mad).

Josh watched fireworks through the window with help from CNA Katie.

Facebook Update:

Sorry for the late update. Yesterday was very busy and eventful.

The family had a meeting with Kevin's medical team Saturday July 3rd. Kevin remains on life support via the ECMO machine and had a tracheostomy Friday to be used in conjunction with the ventilator to help keep his lungs dry and help them heal. The Team feels he can recover from this. However, it may take a significant amount of time for the lungs to clear- perhaps a couple months due to the virus, fluid and inflammation. There's no way to know for sure. So we have to be patient and pray everything goes exactly as it should so that he can come home to us. Please keep praying for another miracle!

We have been blessed with a miracle! We actually talked TO Erin and

SHE TALKED BACK TO US Saturday night!!! She was understandably very hoarse and her voice was very soft. She's still working out the cobwebs from sedation and doesn't know everything about her Dad yet. But it was so wonderful to hear her speak and know that she has come through this ordeal to remain the sweet, loving, witty soul we know and love! She has a long recovery road ahead but now she can get started. She is not able to receive visitors nor answer her own phone. She will eventually have texting ability, but not at this time. You may still direct snail mail to her home address or our address. Please IM if you need information.

7/5/2021

Since Erin is awake Haley and I stopped at St. Mary's to drop off a backpack for Erin. It had her cell phone, charger, notebook, pens, etc. We had to leave it at the front desk since she is still in isolation and have it delivered to her.

Facebook Update:

Josh's Mom visited him this morning and reports a huge turnaround for the good! Staff had him up and walking twice without assistance while using portable oxygen. He seems more alert so she assumed his medications must also have been lowered. He does still tire easily. The doctor told him that if he pushes himself he may be released tomorrow and that is just what he needed to hear! He has his hope back again! He will be staying with his parents for recovery as long as he needs and will then be reachable by phone.

Please continue to pray for Josh and Erin. They both have a way to go for a full recovery.

Mom and I talked to Erin a little bit tonight and she was very happy to say she had passed her swallow test and has been allowed some liquids. As time goes on she will be allowed some solid options, but for now anything is better than ice chips. She was asking the nurse to help her wash her hair tonight- hopefully.

Dad had a rough day. They drained over a liter of fluid from the pleural sac of his right lung via ultrasound guided catheter. They have left it in place for now. We are hopeful that the lessened pressure will allow his lungs a better ability to expand and oxygenate on their own. They didn't say if/when they would do the same to the other lung. They are working to pull additional fluid via a diuretic as well but are cautious to not pull too much at once.

We are taking this all one day at a time and praying for miracle to continue. Thank you everyone for your continued support, prayers and messages.

7/6/2021

Kevin had an ultrasound guided catheter drain in his right lung plural sac and drained over a liter of fluid. Likely caused by fluid overload and ARDS. Left the catheter in place to drain additional fluid- 7 ½ liters over 36 hours. Left lung looked less serious. We would later find out that Kevin had pulled it out somehow. Janyne, the PA (Physician's Assistant) referred to Kevin as some sort of Houdini.

Josh released from hospital to his parents' care.

Scanned Erin's health paperwork to her work office.

Tried calling Erin's cell phone and texting her multiple times. Called nurse's station and had them transfer to her room. No answer, twice.

7/7/2021

Tried reaching Erin again by all methods. No luck. Called Nurse's station a third time and explained that I was not able to reach her and was told that Erin would be unable to answer the phone. When I asked why that was she told me I would have to talk to the charge nurse. She was giving report and would call me when finished. So the worry crept in. Had she had a stroke? Had she become so Hangry they strapped her down-lol? After an hour I became too upset to wait any longer and called back. I was angry now. As it turns out, Erin had suffered profound weakness from her coma and lack of oxygen. She couldn't use her arms or legs, could barely push a call light and could not pick up or hold a telephone. She would end up having to relearn to use her muscles over the course of several weeks through physical and occupational therapy. This was something we were never told and had no idea that she didn't have any of these abilities when she left ICU.

But today she was finally out of isolation. Erin was sat in a chair with hair braided. They asked if Dorene would be coming up to visit. Only one visitor per one calendar day. The same person could leave and come back, but only that one person. Unfortunately, Dorene was not able to see her until the next day. An additional call with the doctor indicated that a visit from her family was very much needed due to her depression.

The doctors wanted to move Erin to Van Matre rehabilitation center early in July, but insurance was unable to provide any coverage for a rehabilitation center.

7/8/2021

I was doing outside chores in anticipation of leaving to go to Madison as soon as Haley got home from work. It was a rather foreboding looking evening, the skies looking stormy. As I was checking out the sky I caught a glimpse of a familiar wingspan overhead. It was the turkey vultures again. There is a small cluster of 8 or 10 that frequent the area seeing what they can scare up in the area. I was always worried about our cats when I see them. We have had a murder of crows harass the squirrel population and take baby squirrels rights out of the nests. I know the vultures are supposed to be scavengers but had heard they were actually bothering live livestock as wildlife has become more scarce over the years, especially with the prevalence of other scavengers like coyotes. Imagine my shock when I looked up again a few moments later and saw over one hundred twenty vultures! Haley was driving in at that moment and we watched the weird flock swirl and dip overhead- seemingly taking their time to hover over our neighborhood. It was unnerving, and felt like a bad omen.

Drove to Madison after Haley and I got off work. She dropped me off at St. Mary's to spend as much time as possible with Erin. She was still unaware of Kevin's and Josh's covid illnesses. I needed to gently break this news to her. I had to assure her that her husband was recovering very well, although not well enough to have called her yet, and that her father was not well, on life support, and that we wanted her to participate in a WebEx call with his doctors the following day.

Needless to say, she was devastated. When I got to the subject of her Dad and said we were meeting with the doctors to discuss what we were going to do, the very first thing she tearfully blurted out was "You aren't going to pull the plug, are you!!?" I assured her that was NOT what we intended going into the meeting.

7/9/2021

Haley spent a few hours with Erin at the hospital in the morning. They visited and Haley got her set up for the Web Ex call, including getting an assistant to sit in to assist her. Haley returned later in the evening to spend several more hours with Erin, when they also Facetimed with dear, dear friends.

1PM – Kevin's care team meeting. Erin, Bob, Sam and Aurora were able to be present via WebEx meeting. Dorene, Haley and Ethan in person. This is the meeting where three doctors, including the chief cardiothoracic surgeon, attempted to strongly persuade us to discontinue Kevin's life support. The entire family was not in agreement with the staff on that subject and elected to buck them on that.

Holy cow! Erin was certainly on the money with her projection of the subject matter. And it was very difficult for her to hear.

I didn't realize that the roller coaster we would be riding would include so many downs from the doctors.

7/10/2021

Waiting for nurse to contact me concerning Kevin's saturation levels being in low 80s today. Will get more information at WebEx later today too.

Dorene and Haley came back to Freeport so Haley could go to a Memorial Concert, where Al (Haley's friend and vocal mentor) was performing with The Usual Suspects, along with some other bands. The memorial concert was dedicated to a friend with whom Haley had had the pleasure of working with through a local house band.

Facebook Update:

Apologies for the late update. We got home from Madison this afternoon and are still regrouping.

Erin had some nice visits this weekend and has started working on being able to use her phone while it is laying on her tray. She is able to eat some solid foods, but is required to have only thickened liquids.

Dad is still heavily sedated but the doctors are happy about the progress of draining made with his chest tube. He is remaining stable.

7/11/2021

Rusty had a seizure a day and a half following his first chemo treatment and was transferred to St. Mary's Hospital in Madison where Erin is at.

7-12-2021

Visited Kevin. Met medical team. Continuing ECMO and taking slightly less aggressive approach to removing fluid as it may have triggered an A-Fib episode. Looking for long term anti-anxiety meds instead of sedatives to combat panic when trying to breathe.

7-13-2021

Erin graduated to thickened liquids and soft solids. Working on hand and finger dexterity. Can pick up phone and is feeding herself. Today she was able to stand and take a couple steps.

Josh doing well. Staying with his parents for extra physical assistance. Still using oxygen.

Facebook Update from Dorene:

I know it has been a few days again, but we like to have something new to tell when we post. And are always hoping for good things to share.

On Monday 7/12 we visited Kevin and met with his medical team. They are continuing ECMO treatment, but taking a slightly less aggressive approach to removing fluid as it triggered an A-fib episode. Fortunately, his body was able to resolve that heart rhythm issue on his own. Because his lungs have not yet improved much, and long-term sedation is not desirable they are working to find correct anti anxiety meds combination. This will aid Kevin and the team in allowing him to be more comfortable as they wake him for physical therapy. This is needed because the ability for intake of breath is greatly limited and will help him deal with the panic. I cannot begin to imagine... We are greatly hopeful this will improve and that the only organ affected will remain the lungs. That gives him a much better chance than having multiple organ involvement. Please continue to pray for the miracle that is clearly needed!

Erin is pushing herself with her physical therapy and improving greatly every day! She has graduated to soft solids, thickened liquids and is pretty much able to feed herself. She is working on hand and finger dexterity and can now pick up her telephone. Texting and dialing are extremely challenging yet. Today she was able to stand and take a couple steps! We should have news soon about where she will be staying for more rehab!

Josh is doing pretty well and is with his Mom and Dad for extra physical assistance during his recovery. He is still using oxygen and doing well at having weaned down and having stayed off the ventilator.

We are so grateful for everyone's continued prayers!

7/14/2021

One of Dorene's coworkers dropped off a gift from Pearl City Zion Church Family – 3 beautifully knitted prayer shawls and 3 handmade wooden prayer crosses, along with a Casey's gas card. This is a church we attended when we lived near Pearl City, for many years but primarily late 1980s- early 2000s. We have stayed in touch with many of those wonderful people. This gift was so overwhelmingly beautiful and heartfelt. Tears of gratitude stream down my (Dorene's) face and my heart is full.

7/15/2021

Pastor Justin made the trek to UW Madison to visit Kevin and was able to spend nearly half an hour with him.

He said he was able to share some encouraging family updates, Erin's favorite Bible verse, and Psalms 23 and Psalms 103. He prayed with Kevin, to encourage him to fight, to have courage and hope in the Lord. Our thanks are inadequate.

Erin was moved to Monroe Hospital for physical therapy and rehabilitation as insurance was inadequate to cover any other type of rehabilitation facility.

Dorene: Now insurance is a very tricky, perplexing and overall frustrating and maddening subject. Erin was carrying the health insurance coverage for she and Josh, and at the highest level of coverage afforded to them. It ends up they have no coverage for any rehabilitative care coverage nor durable home health care supplies, i.e. oxygen, wheelchair, walker, hospital bed rentals, etc…... Now we must scramble to figure out how we are going to continue to provide for them.

Josh had been employed as a driver for a private company that handled delivering COVID test kits to a lab. A few weeks prior to the illnesses Josh had been laid off from his job, as state funding to that company for his position had run out. He had secured a new job at a local factory in shipping and was scheduled to start work on June 21st, the day before he entered the ICU as a patient. He had already pushed back his start date due to Erin's critical illness and his own COVID diagnosis, for which he was already being treated. As time went on, however, the company was unable to hold the position open for Josh, which is understandable. With Erin's job, they were wonderful and absolutely supportive in every way they could be including continuing insurance coverage. Unfortunately, no work, no paycheck.

Josh's Mom posted that Erin was moved to Monroe Hospital for physical therapy today. This will make it so much easier for Josh and family to see her. Erin has been working hard on her physical therapy. She's able to stand unassisted and take more steps unassisted too! She's working hard on getting more strength back in her arms and hands. (Please note that she is still restricted on the number of visitors she can have, so please work with the family if you want to pick a day to see her.)

Josh is still on oxygen but he's making gradual improvement. Each day he's able to do more for himself! Our prayer is that we can get his INR levels in range and that he won't have to take the shots twice a day anymore.

Thank you everyone for all your continued prayers for everyone. We all can feel them! Love all of you.

7/16/2021

Rusty able to come home.
Erin transferred to Monroe Hospital for rehabilitation yesterday

7/18/2021

Facebook Update:

From Mom: Sunday brought the first bit of good news for Kevin in awhile. Although still dealing with some bouts of A-fib and still regularly adjusting sedation medications, progress was made in reducing excess fluid. Additionally, for the first time since he began ECMO treatment, Kevin's lung X-rays show the tiniest bit of improvement! We are so grateful and hopeful this might continue! Thank you for your prayers and support! Please continue to pray for Kevin's continued improvement.

7/22/2021

Dorene took Gary, her Dad, to ER in Monroe. Two days ago, he flipped the old heavy zero turn mower (from the 1970s) over on a bank while mowing, throwing himself off into the gravel. He ended up with a nasty hematoma the size of a brick on his right thigh and a badly cut and bruised elbow, along with a bruised back and waist. Haley visited Erin while Dorene was with their Papa in the ER. Storytime - The farmer in my Dad wouldn't allow himself to go the doctor right away, even though he is on warfarin and risks having internal bleeding from such a trauma. You see, my Mom's cousin (Rusty) who is in hospice care, is living with them during his final life stages and Dad did not want to further complicate things, as he was already disgusted with himself for having misjudged the equipment/ embankment situation. So he delayed the ER visit, hoping the body would not betray him and bruise.

A bright spot from the visit- Erin took first 9 unaided steps with walker. Haley was present to see this. Haley brings smiley face stickers to hospital and gives one to nurse who puts it over her face on her badge.

7/23/2021

Facebook Update from Erin:

Hi everyone! I just wanted to pop in to post a quick update on what is going on with me. I've been discharged from St. Mary's in Madison and have been accepted at Monroe Clinic Hospital to finish my physical and occupational therapy closer to home. This has been so good for my mental health. I have been working hard to get my strength back, and feel a little stronger each day. I have been able to feed myself (sometimes opening things is tough), and I have been able to stand from the wheelchair to a walker a few times now. Today I was even able to march in place for ten steps! Now my left arm just needs to cooperate. It will come with time. I know there is more, but I will try to update more soon. Love you all! Thank you for your continued prayers and all the love and support you've all shown us!

7/24/2021

Kevin has had micro-improvements over the last week. They think he may be approximately halfway through ECMO process. That means probably another 4 weeks before they determine if they are ready to wean him down to just the ventilator, and let lungs do oxygenation for body. He has started to be able to work with ventilator a bit better and get more air in. So able to push more carbon dioxide out on his own and start to clear some of the infiltrates in his lungs. He has been so fortunate that he has only single organ failure but still battling AFIB with those instances being a bit more frequent, lasting longer, and requiring medication now to convert to normal sinus rhythm.

I had been asked repeatedly to assess what Kevin's wishes would be in this situation and had been counseled as to what would happen if the decision were to be made that life support were to be discontinued. It seemed urgent that the decision be made sooner than later. From the perspective of the family of the patient, it seemed to me that the medical staff very much wanted that decision made before the patient regained consciousness. It appeared they were speculating that the patient is not going to survive because they have not met certain "arbitrary" timeline goals. It stood to reason, per my perceived view of that protocol, that if the patient regained consciousness, the family would delay making the decision to discontinue life support, ultimately also delaying the use of that ECMO machine for another potential patient. Since the medical staff initially indicated that it would be at least 9 weeks or more for Kevin to be on ECMO before they expected him to heal, I intended to hold them to that timeline, even if he was not meeting the goals in the timelines they set. That did not please the chief in charge of the ECMO machine, but that was my decision and my family agreed.

Please understand that I am not blind to the need of use of the ECMO machines. But I was quoted a timeline upon admission, and I see nothing that has changed for the worse, overall. I grant that it has not improved. Some of the staff may speak about it in a more grave fashion and say he is failing, but looking at the statistics, point by point, I don't see it. Are there other families who have been blindly led to accept this kind of decision for a loved one because they trusted that was the best decision? Because they were too emotionally overwhelmed to ask questions and look at the details? Was it too soon for that support process to be ended? Certainly, I do not have a medical degree and I didn't wish to start a debate, but it seems that there have been multiple cases that a push to end quickly has occurred. I am asking if it was too soon for that push.

On the flip side, I would NOT want to be in the shoes of the individuals who earn their living by having to make those decisions. I am certain they are making those decisions with the intent of trying to save as many lives as possible with the knowledge they have, and I respect the fact they must do so. It does not mean I will always agree with their decisions.

I took Dad (Gary) back to ER to reevaluate hematoma on thigh. Had developed additional bruising on waist and side. Fortunately, bloodwork indicated the bleeding seems to have stopped. Is to remain in a reclining position. Was really busy at the ER and took around 5 hours. By the time I make the 45 minute trip to take him home I don't think I will have time to make the trip to Madison tonight to see Kevin.

Checked on Erin briefly while at hospital with my Dad.

Rusty has started to run a fever and is barely speaking now. I'm afraid his time may be closer than we thought. Mom stayed with him, and Chad was there to help.

7/27/2021

Facebook Update from Erin:
More victories today! I have been able to stand with the walker

unassisted, and WALK! I walked the rehab gym twice, to the bathroom, and did several stand pivots! Every day I feel a little stronger and can do more. I am over a week ahead on my therapy goals! What a blessing it is! Thank you to everyone who has been there for my family through all of this. We are so thankful and appreciative. Please know how much we love and cherish each of you.

7/29/2021

Working with Erin on getting home health equipment ordered, an arm exercise bike and some other basic supplies.

Kevin often asks for "butt cream" to help the bedsore he had gotten.

Reflection:

Kevin was being treated for a life-threatening infection which had plagued him almost from the beginning of his hospitalization. Persistence and modern medicine finally brought the beast under control. Kevin was not able to verbalize due to having the tracheostomy and could not yet write due to wrist restraints.

Many months after Kevin finally returned home from the hospital, we (including Kevin) actually joked about trying to lip read and us realizing he was saying "butt cream". He has no recollection of the event. Only after seeing clinical photos of the offending infection did we have a new appreciation for his plight.

7/30/2021

Facebook Update from Erin:

Today my midline was removed! A midline is kind of like a pick line but shorter. So this girl is now IV free!

It has been a busy day. I did 6 minutes on the step machine, took a total of 63 steps, did 9 stands (so far!), multiple pivots, and have been able to get upright in bed all by myself! I also did 8 minutes in the arm bike and did OT on my arms. While there is still much weakness, I feel stronger every day and have totally blasted through two weeks of therapy goals! We had to make new ones today. I have been able to mostly dress myself!

They thought I may even be able to be discharged sometime next week at the earliest depending on homecare and outpatient therapy. Thank you to everyone who has been so amazing in showing us love and support during this time. We love you all.

7/31/2021

Face to face meeting with the cardiothoracic team. Dorene, Haley, and Ethan were physically attending with Aurora, Bob, Erin and Sam on Webex. Surprisingly to the Medical Team, Kevin chose today to wake up and be alert. That did not help the medical team's cause, which was to talk strongly to us about discontinuing Kevin's ECMO treatment. After all, the cardiothoracic surgeon oversees that machine, and he makes the call about who gets to use it and for how long! And then when threats seemed to backfire, it was about the quality of life, not the quantity of life- you young people simply do not understand and have no concept of applying these concepts to living. This drew ire from the group as a whole and it was with a great deal of effort the meeting remained civil. Dorene held onto Ethan which kept both seated. Measured words were spoken between clenched teeth. When all was done handshakes were given all around- perhaps much too firmly in one case.

I don't know if anyone else realized that this date is the same date that both Grandma Pat Shores and Michael Terry (Kevin's nephew) passed away and I did not mention it to anyone else involved. I knew when the appointment was made we were in for a rough day just because of the date, but you take the day and time the medical team is available, closest to the family availability....

Ethan stayed to visit with Kevin. We observed through the glass. Kevin smiled and acknowledged Haley but did not wish to look at me and would turn away when I would wave to him. I decided it was best to let the kids visit with him today. He cannot verbalize due to the trach but wanted to badly and managed to force air out enough that he could make a sound- which he is not supposed to do. It can damage his vocal cords and throat. But he desperately wanted to communicate something to us.

Anyone who has gone through it must certainly know what a feeling such circumstances create. But how to describe that hollow numbness, with eye-stinging and a parched throat so dry that you can't swallow because it feels like the sides of your throat will suck in and collapse. And that knot in your gut that sometimes gnaws and sometimes burns, and other times just stabs you for fun…. And you wander around on auto pilot playing out every scenario your mind can conjure, best to worst. And you pray. At first, you pray diligently, then you pray without stopping to actually say "Dear Lord" at the beginning because it is a constant dialogue. Everyone else is certainly tired of hearing you go on about it… Those that continue to listen are your true friends and deserve more than a medal! Even if they truly care, how much should they have to endure? I had often heard it said that we should better not hope that God gives us what we deserve. I certainly felt that this was a time of trial and remember saying "If you want me on my knees, Lord, I'm there!"

8/2/2021

Rusty passed away. The time was short once he knew the chemo was not going to be a viable option. It was only a matter of a couple weeks as his body was in rapid decline. It was SO not fair to him that during his time of need that none of us were able to be there for him as planned because we were all either in a coma with covid or were tending someone who was! Poor Mom had so much to do! Chad helped and Dad had his own issues that compounded the whole affair- not that he wanted to have that problem. I sure hope Rusty knows how much he meant to us all!

8/3/2021

One of the nurses offered to stay in the room with the communication board from 6:30 to 7:05 so that Kevin can tell us what he wants to say. It has been a constant focus of his visits to try to tell us something specific. And he had frustration to the point of extreme agitation, that he cannot convey what is very clearly of utmost importance to him. Usually, by the time we make any headway our visiting time is over or his heart rate is too greatly affected and we have to abandon the visit early. We had been consistently asking the doctors for a speaker valve, which we were told usually isn't terribly successful. I believe since there was such a high mortality rate and Kevin was so critical, they were reluctant to invest resources on someone they were not holding out a great deal of hope for. We had also asked the doctors for other options to try to determine what he may be trying to tell us. We asked about dry erase boards or someone from the clinic who might work with hearing impaired in the hospital who may read lips. None of those options were immediately met with approval. Eventually, a nurse offered a letter board and he was able to spell out a word by pointing. There were only a couple who followed certain doctor's leads and simply indicated the patient was talking due to hallucinations due to heavy sedation and what Kevin was trying to say didn't make sense and meant nothing. Again, I understand that based on other cases and those trends, they were trying to be realistic about the outcome. To us, what mattered was that we were addressing his desire to communicate and that we understand him. Eventually, with his continued survival, family requests and respiratory therapy assistance, Kevin received a speaker valve August 25th.

Dorene meets Grandma Joe and Chad at Garden house after lunch to assess bathroom remodel for Erin and Josh. So many things should happen to make the room and others accessible. But with extremely limited funds we will play carpenters and see what we can accomplish on our own over the next few days. Removing the glass surround and doors, leveling the shower pan, and regluing the surround walls followed by a slight alteration to an arched bath shower rod, 2 shower curtains, a grab bar, a shower chair, and we were in business!

Then it was time to tackle a ramp to the back door. The front elevation left a ramp out of the question. We measured, used as much scrap lumber as we could find and went to work on creating something wide enough for a wheelchair. When that was done, a foundation hole had to be patched and thank goodness my brother and nephew could tackle that- one brain, one brawn.

Another day was a trip to the Durand VFW to borrow a hospital bed, rails, wheelchair, walker and toilet riser. This was a Godsend as insurance didn't cover any durable home medical supplies.

8/5/2021

Message From Erin,

Looks like I may get discharged to home care and outpatient therapy tomorrow! God is so good!

8/6/2021

Erin came home from the hospital for the first time. The staff provided the most beautiful send off of volunteers, staff and even patients!

I stopped at the Clinic Supply Store and purchased a gait belt to assist in helping move and escort Erin.

8/7/2021

Facebook Update from Dorene:

This week has seen many ups and downs. The week began with a wonderfully awake and alert Kevin, who was able to interact and do some communication via a word board. He actively participated in physical and occupational therapy, and made it clear his desire was to heal and get home.

Unfortunately, that wakeful phase was short-lived as a major SVT (supraventricular tachycardia) heart incident caused him to have an electrical intervention when medication failed to bring his heart back into normal sinus rhythm- twice, a little later in the week. Now we are sort of back to where we were prior to the beginning of the week.

Despite all of the positive communication we have had we are still hoping for positive signs of lung improvement. They aren't yet apparent. Please continue to pray for healing.

Thank you for your prayers of love and support for our family.

8/9/2021

Please do not misinterpret the following statements. They are not intended to discredit any clergy members. This was an extraordinary time, unprecedented, with restrictions for access to patients. Kevin and I were not regular attendees at any church at that time, although our daughters and son-in-law were. And these pastors made extra efforts in so many ways, as did the elders, other support staffs and congregations of these churches. So did countless other churches, pastors, congregations, chaplains, and many, many that are completely unknown to us, yet today!

Early in Kevin's stay Pastor Justin was able to visit Kevin. However, following was their family vacation, church camp, personal covid, Session (regional church related) meeting, immediate family covid... This truly prevented him from making personal revisits.

We had made multiple requests for clergy to visit Kevin from UW Hospital. However, this did not happen- presumably due to not wanting to risk exposure to and spread of the virus with additional staff members.

Dorene contacted Apostle Mike to ask if he would be able to pay a pastoral visit to Kevin. Unfortunately, he and his wife were leaving for California for a church opening the following day and wouldn't return until Sunday night. On Sunday night there were severe thunderstorms in Chicago and their flight was diverted to Dallas where they had to wait until Monday evening for another flight. His intent was to anoint Kevin and pray a specific prayer for his healing. The flight delay and the recent travel made it impossible for him to be there.

We began to feel that any efforts we made for spiritual support were being thwarted by a dark force. These weren't the only occasions such events occurred. Look at the day we tried to come home to Kevin and the tree blocked or path, delaying us. Take the next day, for example....

8/11/2021

On August 11th, Erin was finally going to be able to see Kevin in the TLC Unit at UW Madison. She was released from the hospital maybe a bit early, as Kevin was not seen as improving. We were being told by doctors and staff that he was declining and we were fearful that she needed to get there to see him as soon as possible lest she lose her chance.

Upon getting ready to leave for UW, Erin fell in the kitchen at her house, and was not strong enough to be able to get up from the floor.

After an hour or more of Haley, Josh, Dorene, and Ethan tugging and pulling to try to get her up off the floor, they decided it was time to call the fire department for assistance.

Five big guys and three smaller ones showed up at the house, placed that newly purchased gait belt around her, and had her up in .2 seconds. They placed her into a wheelchair, and then wheeled her down the ramp on the side of the house. They helped her get into the vehicle, and then got her situated so we could be on their way to UW. Fortunately, she was not injured more than some bruising.

Along the way, Dorene called the TLC unit at UW to verify whether we could get the meeting rescheduled for 2pm instead of 1pm. They said it was a go, so we continued on our way.

One third of the way there the group encountered a deer who decided to race the vehicle, then when we stopped, it stopped. Then it finally opted not to cross the road anyway.

Dorene and Erin were the only ones allowed to enter the hospital due to COVID limitations on visitors – Erin as a visitor and Dorene as her chaperone. With Kevin's health deteriorating, they wanted to make sure Erin was able to see him. They were about to sit in on a meeting with Kevin's care team to discuss his treatment and condition.

They were ushered into a room with some chairs and a couch, and a screen for WebEx meetings. Present were Nurse Coordinators (liaisons between the nursing staff and the families), an RN who had been caring for Kevin from the beginning, current rotation Doctors, along with Erin and Dorene. Ethan, Josh, Haley, and Aurora were listening via a WebEx meeting from various locations. It was discussed that Kevin's health future was unknown, and that they were in uncharted territory with his care; they had never had someone on ECMO as long as Kevin was, especially someone of his age. We were wading in uncertain waters.

At one point, Ethan spoke up. He'd been given some feedback from a certain cardiothoracic surgeon, who'd stated rather bluntly that he was being immature, and that he needed to be realistic about Kevin's chances at survival and recovery. It was stated that as Kevin's children, we could not possibly understand the severity of his illness, and that it was about quality over quantity. We needed to understand that he, as a doctor, had the medical opinion to make such decisions. The next person who should be making those decisions would be Dorene.

Ethan stated that while he *did* understand the gravity of the situation, he also knew who his father was. He said, "[Kevin] is the strongest man I know. Yes, I understand that the situation does not look good, but I refuse to give up hope for him. He is still fighting, and we are going to continue to let him fight as long as he wants and can. I'm not being immature or in denial. I know what's happening. But I am not going to give up hope." By the time we were done with the meeting, many of the people in the meeting room had tears in their eyes. They could see -how much Kevin meant to his family, and how hard they were fighting for him.

8/13/2021

Friday the 13th – Kevin has bronchoscopy scheduled later today. Hoping for answer to cough.

8/14/2021

Memorial Service for Rusty this morning. Gathering at funeral home, then lunch at Mom and Dad's following.

Received call from UW Hospital staff doctor for what is supposed to be a daily update, on the way to the Memorial Service. At this point, I have not received a call from the NP doing case management, for several days. I had previously been told I am too involved in Kevin's care and "do not need to act as a primary care provider", that my micromanaging and reviewing medical decisions the TEAM has made, after the fact, is not productive for anyone. However, since this is a University Hospital teaching facility and doctor/ intern staff rotates every two weeks, I feel greatly compelled to be certain that each time there is a staff change, I review his case with the onboarding staff as I want to be sure pain management is addressed. As you may recall, Kevin has an unusually high tolerance to pain medication and therefore, I want to be sure they are aware of that fact and the degree of that issue.

One would think and hope that charts and histories are thoroughly read on a patient. But this is real world where emergencies and situations happen that sometimes cause the incorrect decisions to occur. I wanted to be sure I continued to have valid input regardless of whether I was physically present onsite. I recognize that there was concern for my mental health during this ordeal, however my concern was for the medication regimen being used for Kevin.

Additionally, I was asking questions concerning the use of specific drugs used to control heart rhythm, diuretics, etc., and why they were or were not continuing to be used in situations that kept presenting themselves. It would seem to a layperson that if a situation presents repeatedly, it may make a case for the use of a specific protocol.

Another concern was attempting to wean Kevin from the use of heavy-duty sedatives required to keep him calm while under the suffocating feeling of the ventilator. He needed to be awake enough to be able to breathe on the ventilator when they weaned him from the ECMO machine. Therefore, it was important to stop the heavy-duty sedatives and try switching to a long-term SSRI/ antidepressant, as he continued to be highly agitated. It seemed that certain medications caused Kevin to have more hallucinations and bad dreams. Kevin had briefly taken a similar prescription when dealing with insomnia in the past, and he had experienced Serotonin Syndrome, reporting that the drug had caused him to feel like his brain was on fire. Now, when he could not speak for himself I wanted to be his voice. We had witnessed Kevin try to pull his restrained arm away from a nurse who was trying to administer bedtime sedatives (this was prior to SSRI administration). Despite repeatedly discussing these potential adverse reactions, the team felt there were limited options available (due to many medications interfering with his heart rhythms) and proceeded with the trial of those medications, which did not achieve the desired results. Following a consult with Psychiatry, new options were identified. One of the new options, ketamine, was likely to be well tolerated. We eventually found that this medication seemed to be having a reverse effect on his behavior. The more they attempted to administer the worse he behaved! I'm not so sure that some of the other heavy sedatives didn't also produce those results, in hindsight. Eventually the adjustments resulted in being able to wean him off heavy sedatives. (But that did not occur until later in early September. And because the TEAM could not determine whether his agitation was due to trying to wean him from the ventilator and he was having a breathing issue, or whether it was some type of sedative medication issue, or a combination the decision to push forward with the weaning process had to sometimes be slowed, as his heart did not cooperate.

Through mid-August and September I had the luxury of working with several new TEAM members, (as well as several existing TEAM members). Here I want to give a shout out to an outstanding Physician's Assistant. I would have been completely lost without her; and the amazing ECMO Team who were so invested in Kevin they were like family; and several of the nursing staff who were especially standouts among the highly qualified, superior team of nurses. These nurses gave more than I knew was possible. I have seen families whose members give far, far less- and we come from a family who is very giving and expect others to be the same. Somehow this analogy isn't adequate. You don't understand what I am trying to convey here. These nurses and ECMO Team and PA couldn't have had anything left of themselves when they left their shifts at the hospital- they were that giving! Yet I know all of them have lives outside of this vocation! And this was DEEP into the period of the pandemic. Yet all I saw was a willingness to suit up in the mountains of PPE, looking like they were astronauts with the helmets (hoods) and visors, hoses, suits, gloves, etc. to enter a restricted, viral contaminated room and carefully tend to my husband's needs.

Since the last TEAM meeting, it has been made clear that Kevin is not progressing toward recovery. And the explanation from the nurse on duty following the bronchoscopy indicated Kevin had no secretions blocking the airways, only scar tissue which had developed. I was hoping for a little more thorough discussion with a doctor, but unfortunately, there was not a great deal of additional information concerning the bronchoscopy.

Erin and Josh attend Memorial Service and Erin requires a fair amount of assistance to navigate, understandably. By lunchtime she tells us she has a lump on her upper thigh and Josh takes her to the ER for evaluation.

Erin is readmitted to hospital with bad cellulitis infection in upper right leg.

To Haley from Mom for consideration to post as Facebook update:

This week wasn't quite as rough for Kevin from the standpoint of his heart functions. The medical team met with us on Wednesday and let us know that they had been trying to wean Kevin incrementally form the ECMO machine. Thus far, his lungs do not have the capability to assume any of those tasks. A bronchoscopy was done yesterday to identify potential obstructions or excess secretions noted in his X-ray. Although final results are not in, it appears that the lung tissue itself has turned to fibrous scar tissue. This is what can happen in COVID pneumonia. When the body beats the infection, it goes through an inflammatory stage. Then it isn't a matter of whether the body is necessarily strong enough to beat it. He is still very strong, physically. No one in modern science-based medicine that is operating out of a government reimbursed hospital has a solution for the cytokine storm that has caused this inflammatory response and resulting scarring - destroying lung tissue. Bless the CDC and their paid protocol.

8/15/2021

At this point only a miracle will save him as we are told that he is declining and his lungs have shown little to no signs of improvement during this time on ECMO, which would have been prime healing time- the time all previous patients showed healing. We have seen his strong body successfully beat the infectious stage of the disease. Now we continue to watch him struggle through the inflammation stage of the disease. But instead of recovery to the soft and elastic lung tissue he once had, we see the aftermath of fibrous scar tissue develop that is not allowing his lungs the ability to expand and contract, thus limiting his ability for oxygen exchange- breathing.

This is the phase where no more healing is possible now, we are told. We are told he isn't eligible for lung transplant.

They are working to try to wean him off ECMO, the machine that extracts then externally oxygenates, filters and returns his blood back to his body to keep his organs and tissues - him- alive. His lungs, even with a ventilator cannot sustain his life, even short term.

This means he can never leave the hospital to experience the world outside his glass-doored cubicle again. I wish that I could take him outside, just once more.

8/16/2021

Erin begins having swelling of face and shoulders. Still in hospital.

8/17/2021

Erin has Cushing's Disease.

Somewhere around this time Dorene is contacted by the UW School of Medicine Blood Bank. As Kevin is a long term survivor of covid, and perhaps they do know the strain, but are not sharing that information, they are asking for permission to draw an additional 1 tablespoon of blood from Kevin for research purposes. Only microdroplets would ever be used at any time for their research so the quantity of 1 tablespoon is actually a large quantity they tell me. For this I grant permission and sign the release forms and return them so that they can proceed.

8/18/2021

Coworkers and friends all showed up at Erin and Josh's ready to work. A coworker's friend owned an aluminum ramp and we all met to set it up for Erin. My brother and I had assembled a plywood ramp for short term use to get Erin home and in and out for the interim. So these friends had the task of deconstruction before they could install the new ramp, making for a more cumbersome project. Here is yet another case of gracious assistance by all involved where help was needed!

8/20/2021

Erin is released home the second time.

8/21/2021

Kevin is in a new room in TLC that has a bank of windows for natural sunlight. Unfortunately, his room heats to around 85 degrees, which maintenance has not been able to solve, and is complicated by heat generated by his machines. The creative nursing team has improvised with traditional ice packs and have located a nifty water blanket that recirculates water and cools to temperature you desire. Hopefully this will help.

8/22/2021

The Cardiothoracic team made changes on ECMO machine and ventilator today. Kevin tolerated well. This is second attempt at weaning. The first attempt was a month ago and not enough healing had occurred yet to proceed, so process was postponed. One of Kevin's biggest challenges recently is that he has been very agitated. He is overall less sedated now as they work on some physical therapy and ECMO weaning again. Unfortunately, the agitation has slowed the weaning process, as it is sometimes unclear as to whether his agitation is due to difficulty breathing or some other issue. Therefore, we pray that he remains calm although I know that he is so bored and lonely. There are staff members who try to keep him company as they can fit it into their schedule. Hospital policy dictates that since he was admitted as a COVID patient, he will be a COVID patient for the duration of his entire hospitalization regardless of the length of stay, be it two months or a year. This means under current COVID guidelines, Kevin may only have one visitor for thirty minutes, up to twice per week but not in the same day. The hospital administration and I have vastly different views on this topic. However, no resolution in my favor has been realized at this time. And if COVID causes more shutdowns, these guidelines may become more restrictive, as they have been previously. Doesn't mean we will not continue to plead our case, as we feel he would benefit from that support.

8/23/2021

During a WebEx call Kevin's youngest brother Bob and Dorene are trying to talk to Kevin about his somewhat agitated and aggressive behavior as of late. Bob is asking him if he is going to behave and as we await a nod or some response, the i-pod screen starts turning away from Kevin so we are no longer able to see him. We realized then that he had no longer wanted to be lectured and had used his foot to push the screen away. Bob and I both laughed out loud at this. Bob said that it was at least clear what his answer was! Eventually, he pulled the screen back toward himself and we visited a bit longer until evening rounds began.

8/25/2021

Have been talking to Kevin. He had speaker valve in temporarily. Very emotional today. He broke down and cried after nurses left. It takes a lot of air, and I can't make out a lot over the microphone because of how it comes in bursts. Breathing is better today, though. Dorene reassured Kevin he was still very much loved, and he has calmed down and rested. Talked about it being okay to be mad and sad and have momentary pity parties, then regroup and move forward. Haley said it might be extra hard for Kevin because he doesn't have that internal dialogue to help talk through it. (Dad has a different way of viewing things where he sees pictures, videos, images, maps, graphs, etc.)

His nurse said they were going to let Dorene go from the WebEx call because Kevin's heart rate was still running too high, and that they were giving him medication to slow his heart rate. He'd been resting for about 30 minutes. Hearing his own voice had triggered an emotional state, which had caused his heart rate to increase to an A-fib episode. They took the speaker valve out and explained to Kevin it was because he was tired so as not to worry him further. He later converted back to a normal sinus rhythm. Will take him his cell phone on the next trip so he can listen to Chicago Bears Nation.

8/26/2021

As the fundraiser t-shirts said, "prayer works, COVID sucks, love heals". And it appears to be true. Your prayers and love are having a tremendous impact on Kevin. Over the past week, more effort and progress has been made on weaning from the ECMO machine.

8/28/2021

7:42 pm – I called for hotel driver to pick me (Dorene) up from the UW hospital to go back to Best Western after visiting Kevin.

8/30/2021

Haley finishes phase 1 of COVID Ribbon Tattoo.

8/31/2021

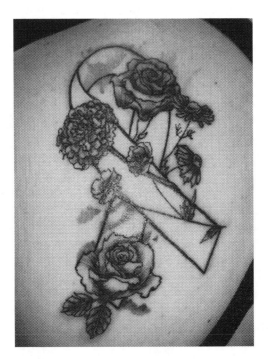

COVID Ribbon Tattoo Shading finished.

9/3/2021

Dorene: Had Kevin's ECMO nurse from TLC contact me. She said he is extremely agitated and we are hoping if you talk to him you will be able to calm him down. Normally, she was one of the staff who could do the most with him. I spent about 8 hours on the phone and i-pad with him with only a couple breaks to make a couple other inquiries.

Due to Kevin's constant agitation the staff had been forced to restrain him. And not only had they had to restrain his wrists, also his ankles. The medications for calming and sedation were not having the desired effect. I spent an hour walking around outside showing him the flowers, garden, birds, etc. But he wasn't easily distracted from his agitation. Now he was telling me there were people hiding behind the pillar in the room and that they were trying to kill him, and that if I didn't get him out of there tonight he was as good as dead! He was visibly fearful, this man who I've not seen fearful of much in life. He was fighting his restraints and peering off camera at an unknown foe while begging me to help him. I kept trying to reassure him that no one was there, that the TLC nurse would help him. He then told me she was the one trying to kill him.

If you watch enough crime tv you will have seen at least one show about a mercy killing nurse. Good Lord! Could he be telling the truth? How would I know? I had to get Haley to talk to him while I called the TLC unit on another phone to talk to the nurse and find out what was going on. My gut told me she wasn't a killer. I explained about his paranoia and that if possible maybe a different nurse could cover the final round of the shift so as not to further upset him. By then he was asking for me again.

He hadn't calmed down. Now he was convinced even the staff members he is closest to were trying to kill him. He insisted I needed to find another hospital to move him to immediately. I told him I had been trying to find another hospital, but that he required very specific equipment and a helicopter, and that all other hospitals were completely full- probably not a lie. After a time, he seemed to resolve himself to the fact that nothing could be done and fortunately, the next shift distracted him with rounds and I was able to let them take care of him. It was an awful feeling to be far away and have him in such a panicked state and not be able to do anything to help him, not even be able to verify his concerns were unwarranted in person- although I was confident they were unwarranted. But, I couldn't be there for him. It was yet another time covid restrictions kept up apart.

9/4/2021

Dad paranoid of Mom's whereabouts. Dad had bad paranoia day, and Mom on phone with Dad for several hours throughout the day. Must constantly know where Mom is. WebEx call he kept asking where she was. Had to see her.

Kevin managed to pull his arterial line out somehow and tear the palm of his hand open. Big mess. After that battle he now is also sporting protective mittens on his hands due to his agitation.

9/6/2021

Kevin has been working UW Madison's Cardiothoracic and Pulmonary staff hard. He is uncharted territory as they haven't had another COVID patient with single organ failure who has survived to this point and has yet to be weaned from ECMO. One would think that would be a positive, yet it seems to present its own challenges. There have been multiple ups and downs over the past few weeks during what we thought would be the last short phase of weaning. Yet, here we are, still on ECMO. He has battled so many issues including heart rhythm, insomnia, confusion from sedation, agitation and depression, and disappointment, but he's still anxiously looking forward to the next phase of recovery.

9/7/2021

Renewal of vows. For a couple of days, Kevin had made it known that he wanted to renew his and Dorene's wedding vows.

Becky, Jill and Stephanie from ECMO, Andrew O and several others worked hard to arrange this for us. One of the girls ran a bouquet of life-like white roses into Dorene before it started. Many staff stood outside of Kevin's room looking in through the glass. So much went into this in a short time. The kids were with us on WebEx, other family members who routinely joined Webex meetings attended. I brought the white leather zippered bible I received for Christmas when I was 8 from my Grandparents. It was complete with music by Haley and vows by Josh. I wanted to look pretty and wore makeup but I needn't have bothered - that room was 95 degrees and the face shield didn't help. That, and the fact Kevin wanted to be sure that I and all of his family understood his wishes for me to be happy and live life to the fullest if he were not to make a recovery. I know this was very important to him to convey but caught me completely off guard, causing me to be a basket case. How can you say thank you to someone who loves you so much other than to promise to honor their wishes. But I wasn't ready to let go yet.

9/8/2021

Kevin pulmonary testing done.

9/10/2021

I had the most wonderful surprise today! Mick and Diane dropped in and caught me as I was heading back to work after a late lunch! They are past coworkers of Kevin's and we are decades-long friends. They have been an important sounding board for Haley and I throughout this whole ordeal. Such wonderful friends.

Facebook Update from Dorene:

I had to share that my Love has had a wonderful week! Kevin has made amazing strides in all areas and has been strong in mind, body and spirit. He has been using the speaking valve successfully- how beautiful to hear his voice! In physical therapy he has been sitting on the edge of the bed, building core strength and preparing to work toward the next goal of standing and using a walker! He slept well last night and it made such a wonderful difference for him- and we believe since he has required less medicines that has certainly been in his best interest.

The speaking valve and the physical therapy gets him closer to being able to wean off ECMO. That lung, vascular and muscle strength play together!

Thank you for your continued prayers! It makes all the difference in our lives and in his recovery! We could not imagine our lives without the words of encouragement you have sent. It always seems to come at just the right time!

We thank God for all of you- you are such blessings to us!

9/11/2021

Haley and I were able to see Sam and family today! We have missed them so much

9/16/2021

Kevin able to start texting, often with nurse Megan's help. Kevin has asked Dorene about a settlement he should be receiving from the Peoria Police Department after "the shooting." Confused, Dorene asked him what he meant. He said he was on the police force, and that there had been an investigation because he ended up shooting a bad guy. They'd just settled after a year-long investigation, and he thought he should be receiving a settlement check. They'd put him on administrative leave and took his gun while the investigation was going on. He asked Dorene to check the mail to see if it had arrived. Dorene told him she'd look for this check to appease him, as she was not ready to tell him this was not a real event, and that it was likely one of his delusions.

Texted Haley asking if she could make strawberry pop. She said with carbonated water. Kevin said, "Do It!" Haley told Dorene she thought he was getting a little bossy.

Kevin is asking about his car wondering where it was. Dorene tells him it's safe and sound in the garage. He asks for a picture of it because he believes it has been stolen. He again asks Dorene to investigate him getting administrative leave pay from the police department from when he was placed on leave for a shooting he had while on duty a year ago. Asked her to find the letter that was sent explaining it was settled. Dorene realized at this point there were still issues with Kevin's mental state and they weren't out of the woods yet. Dorene was very concerned as she didn't know if this was still a short term issue or would be a long term issue we would be dealing with.

He's asking us to make everyone understand he wasn't in the military. We asked him if he thought people thought he was and he said yes. (Kevin had delusions about a funeral for a man in the military and thought people got the impression he served as well).

Facebook Update from Dorene:
Thank you again everyone for your love and prayers!
Kevin continues to improve, though if you know Kevin personally you will know that he is not satisfied with the rate of speed he is moving. I keep

reminding him that he has really only been managing his own recovery for less than 2 weeks. That is when the meds that kept him sedated were stopped and he was able to start having cognitive conversations/ thoughts AND start serious physical therapy in which he participated!! He STOOD this week!!! With the walker and aides. But he STOOD!!

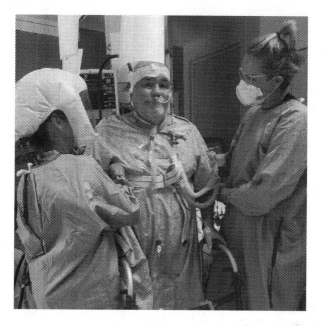

He had swallow tests already!! He passed one of two! He can actually have thickened liquids and soft foods! Most folks in his position do not pass this test this early. It is incredible how much he has accomplished in such a short time.

He is still on ECMO, but on low settings, allowing his lungs time to heal and the muscular and vascular and cardiac systems to gain strength. I know that with his determination and a little more time practicing the swallowing techniques he will soon be able to pass the liquid swallow test, too! Then he can fully enjoy a glass of ice water or some Diet Coke (the nectar of the gods, as he proclaims). He is actually able to have tiny spoonfuls of these precious commodities now, but it certainly isn't the same as being able to take a drink when you feel so thirsty.

And get this- Infectious Disease has granted me permission to actually not wear gloves the next time I am with Kevin- I can finally hold hands with my sweetheart!

He is learning to use a speaking valve, but it is not something that is in use all the time, and not something he has control of usage. Respiratory Therapy is in control of when and for how long he is able to use the device as the ventilator pressure setting have to be adjusted to accommodate. So he isn't able to take telephone calls.

He is not ready to deal with social media yet. His days are very busy and scheduled, and it is a hospital, so unfortunately it isn't always a place where sleep comes easily., despite their best efforts. He truly appreciates hearing that you have all sent wishes, as his nurses often read the comments to him. I do read cards and a daily devotional with him on out Webex i-pad visit each day.

Now that Kevin is awake, alert and working hard to achieve his goals, if anyone wishes to send a note to him on this site they are welcome to! If you wish to send a physical card to our home and need the address, just let us know. We will hand deliver the cards to him weekly.

Thank you again for your love and well wishes!!

9/21/2021

ECMO lines are out, and blood gasses are looking good. Stopped using ventilator, breathing on his own just using oxygen. Could be moved out of ICU by end of week. I am so incredibly elated! It has finally come to pass after all the trials he has gone through!

9/22/2021

Kevin has been moved to Intermediate care. There was a parade for him by the TLC Unit as he was wheeled out. It was beautiful, wish I could have been there for it!

9/23/2021

So, apparently, my husband has been moved to the covid wing of the hospital! He is now in isolation and can have NO VISITORS! We are livid! It's like a giant slap in the face to have survived this ordeal, be given the okay by the Infectious Disease Team to actually reduce PPE protocol, only to have him "graduate" and place him in a location that prohibits physical contact. It's almost like jail to someone who is dealing with something akin to PTSD from having been weaned from a ventilator, and is not even physically mobile! The doctor that has been assigned Kevin's case and other staff are puzzled and trying to rectify this. But I believe it keeps coming back to, same admission as a covid patient therefore you remain a covid patient until discharge. Again, I believe it is all insurance and government reimbursement related. Hopefully, he will only be here a couple days before moving to Select Rehabilitation Hospital, because I am powerless to do anything about this, it seems.

9/24/2021

Not only is he in isolation, they are greatly understaffed in that ward. He is lucky to see one face a couple times briefly during a shift. They do their jobs proficiently when there, but they are stretched to their limits. There is supposed to be physical therapy and occupational therapy being performed and that has yet to happen. He hasn't even been allowed to be assisted to get out of bed to sit in a chair by the end of Day 3. And when a representative from Select Hospital went to UW to get Kevin to sign forms for admission to Select they refused entrance to her because of the isolation ward which really complicated things. I ended up having to give permission as he still doesn't have vocalization ability all the time, nor the dexterity or fine motor skills to even sign his name yet.

After a few days here being with much less contact than in TLC it has become more apparent that he still has not regained all of his mental acuity. He is also emotionally fragile. There are several things he and I discussed previously that I was certain he was aware of and he was not. For example, and this is the big one, Erin had covid and was in a coma for almost a month! The onset was prior to him getting sick. When I tried to talk to Kevin about it, he flat out refused to accept it as the truth, as though he were trying to negate the event by refusing to acknowledge it. When I finally convinced him, he was grief-stricken. He and Erin communicated be texts and spoke at length later that evening and it was very helpful for both of them. Of course, he also did not know about Josh also having had covid. After the toll this had taken on him, I could not tell him about two other family members and a close friend who had died during his illness. That would have to wait for awhile yet.

9/26/2021

To say Kevin is chomping at the bit to get out of UW would be an understatement. He is really feeling lonely and depressed and anxious, and fears that all he gained in the way of rehabilitation in TLC has been lost over the past week while waiting for a bed at Select. Yesterday he talked them into getting him out of bed to sit in a chair for a little while. A hard plastic cardiac chair was the available option, not ideal for a recovering bedsore bottom. They then left him there for over an hour after telling him they'd get back to him when they had time. I know he is frustrated and lonely. I wish I could do something to make this transition to the new facility happen faster.

Each day we read our daily devotional together, try to reflect on the good and hope the next day will be a positive step forward.

9/28/2021

Facebook Update from Dorene:

Kevin has been doing great. He will be moving out of UW Madison hospital to Select Specialty Hospital in Madison sometime this week- as soon as the next bed becomes available. This is projected to be a short preparatory stay of maybe only a week or two. Then it's on to Van Matre Rehabilitation in Rockford IL to finish his rehab before heading HOME!!!!!

We can't wait for that day!

If you want to snail mail anything send it to the home address and we will deliver it to him as we will now get to see quite regularly!

Thank you for all your prayers and well wishes! It has made all the difference for our family! Much love to you all!

9/29/2021

Meeting Kevin at Select Specialties.
Arrived at 1:00 pm and he arrived about 3:00 pm.

Facebook Update by Dorene:
After 99 days- It's moving day! FINALLY!! I am meeting Kevin at his new digs around 1:15 pm today if all runs on time!! Here he comes Select Hospital Rehab!

From Erin:
I just took 51 steps, did the step bike for 5 minutes and multiple stand and pivots! Now that PT is done for the day, it is time for OT to work on my arm muscles! Let's do this!

Daddy asked me to post that he is going to be moving to Select Hospital in Madison today after 99 days at UW! He asks that we all pray he does well there so he can to Van Matre for rehab! We are so happy! Thank you all for your love, support, and prayers. They mean so much to us!

10/3/2021

We have already begun work on tearing off the old deck and steps to our driveway entrance to the house, so that we can reconfigure for a wheelchair ramp and deck. We ended up tearing out my south facing flowerbed too and were able to keep the exact same footprint by wrapping the ramp around the house using that space. It would end up taking us until a day or so before Kevin got home (October 27) to finish up everything that needed to be done. But that's what happens when you are DIYers working with limited labor and funds- lol. But it gives you a great sense of accomplishment. We could never have accomplished this without my Mom and Dad, brother and cousin.

Kevin is not only able to sit on the bedside, but can transfer to his chair with his walker! He is working on building to a cap trial with his tracheotomy using just supplemental oxygen using the nasal cannula.

Select Hospital staff is great, and we are looking forward to getting Kevin's respiratory therapy in order, as well as PT and OT before moving on to Van Matre or even home!

Thanks for your continued love and prayers!

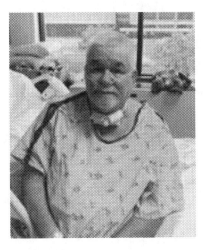

10/5/2021

Kevin takes his first steps in the hallways of Select.
Erin and Josh visit Kevin at Select

10/7/2021

Facebook Update from Erin:
This past week I started Occupational Therapy, which is for my arms. I can tell you, my arms are tired- lol! This coming week I have a couple stress tests and an echocardiogram to make sure everything is okay, as my

heartbeat has been a bit high. I then start Physical Therapy the following week to help strengthen my legs. It looks like I will have approximately 12 weeks of OT and at least 6 weeks of PT. The Cushings Syndrome seems to be starting to correct itseld since I am off the dexamethasone steroid, and am combatting the hair loss with vitamins and hair care. I told Josh I would huge arms muscles after all this therapy!

10/9/2021

Ethan and Aurora visit Kevin. This is first time Aurora has gotten to see Kevin in person since he was admitted to the hospital.

10/10/2021

Facebook Update from Dorene:

This is our first hug with Kevin being able to stand up unassisted!!!! The first of so many more sweet moments to come in our lives! So lucky and thankful to have each other!

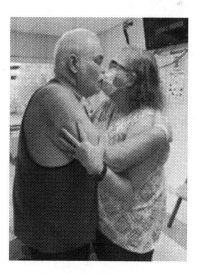

10/11/2021

Trach is finally out after 4 months.

It is around this time that Kevin is able to start using his phone well enough to start using social media. I needed to bring him up to date on the loss of family and friends while he had been ill. Rusty was the first loss I felt he needed to know about. It was difficult for him, but at least he had a spark in the back of his mind to draw from, that there had been an illness. Then one of his best friends, who had been a coworker for many years, had died from the very illness Kevin had just lived through. This was a tough loss to accept as he was living the horror. He had also lost another family member who was young, and it was quite unexpected- such a tragedy! There were other losses, but none so close, and they could wait for another day. This had taken a tremendous toll emotionally. At least I didn't have to worry about him finding out on Facebook about loved ones whom we had lost.

10/15/2021

Still sitting at Select waiting for a bed at Van Matre. Insurance delay caused us to miss out on the last bed availability… Frustration.

10/17/2021

Kevin walking unassisted! He is doing so well, even if he doesn't feel he is…

10/19/2021

Leaving Select for Van Matre. Finally! It's much later in the afternoon than originally planned, but that is normal in this transport business I have found. I meet Kevin at the front door and accompany the EMTs and Kevin, in his gurney, to his new room! We are into the home stretch!

10/20/2021

I show up at Van Matre for the tour and review of the rehabilitation program. Unfortunately, I missed the actual physical rehab sessions due to other commitments this morning. But this is an amazing facility, and he is really upbeat!

Facebook Update from Kevin:

Day 1 at Van Matre is in the books. I'm sore, my back is stiff and I'm tired. But feel like I have accomplished what I wanted day 1 to be.

Everyone was surprised how well I did. With my history they expected someone much less mobile and alert.

I can see how they get people in condition so quickly.

10/21/2021

Facebook Update from Kevin:

Got a special visitor tonight. I haven't seen her in person since June- Haley.

She did visit me when I was asleep but I don't remember that.

10/26/2021

Facebook Update from Kevin:

My therapy Angels from Van Matre are Dr. K, Krista my case manager, Kalil and Steve my physical therapy guys, among others.

They have fine-tuned me to be capable in a home environment. They all have been so understanding of my journey and pushed me further than I thought I could go. With the help from these Angels, I am scheduled for discharge Wednesday at 10:00 am.

Yes! I'm going home. I cry just thinking about it.

So much has changed.

10/27/2021

Facebook Update:
Dad came HOME today!!!

EPILOGUE

So much of what was posted on Facebook remained somewhat generic, but we tried our best to be upbeat and positive. Because a thankful heart IS a happy heart. No one wanted bad news all the time. When prayer requests were needed they were asked for, but some things were simply too personal to share. The constant throughout was that we were so very grateful for all of the support everyone gave without hesitation! Some days it was the only way we powered through.

We also learned that, fortunately, we do not need to have a member of clergy present in order to pray effectively. Maybe we needed to be reminded that God is right here and doesn't require a special "tool" to access. And each of us has the opportunity to help each other more than we realize, simply by being a positive light in another's life every chance we get.

We were shown there is great power in numbers. And there were countless people who, regardless of denomination or creed, sent their prayers and pleas, good ju-ju and vibes, and positivity! It was sent to or on behalf of our family members, people they maybe didn't even know. And it made all the difference in their recovery! And it certainly helped those of us who struggled watching them struggle!

For that we thank you and send our love in return! And we pray that God will bless you as he has blessed us!

THE AUTHORS

This book was written by Kevin Shores, Erin Shores Dietz, Dorene Abels Shores, and Haley Shores. We lived the story you're about to read. It's raw and real.

Kevin was born in Northwestern Illinois, but due to his Dad's roofing business, grew up in southern California. He is a retired Manufacturing Manager, and now enjoys raising show pigeons.

Erin was born and raised in Northwestern Illinois, and still lives there to this day. She is currently a Training Specialist, and enjoys pens, stickers, writing letters, and knitting scarves.

Dorene was born in Northwestern Illinois, and recently retired from the USDA after 39 years of service. She is a pillar of strength and the family Matriarch.

Haley was born in Northwestern Illinois, and now lives in Southern Wisconsin. She is a Systems Validation Analyst who enjoys showcasing her musical talent and her cats and dog.

Printed in the United States
by Baker & Taylor Publisher Services